FIRST LIGHT

THE MAKING OF A HEALER: RECLAIM YOUR LIFE,
YOUR POWER, YOUR DESTINY

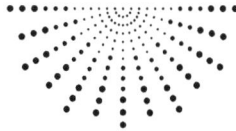

ISA LARA MARIÉ

AMA PUBLISHING   OPEN CROWN

CONTENTS

ACKNOWLEDGEMENT

All that I am chooses to Acknowledge.
all Beings in consensual reality and those
that Dream elsewhere.

For all those who kept me alive and sane.

For the children and all those touched by an unwanted hand. For the Ones who cannot speak.

For Leta Rose and Walter Crinnion

For the Great Mother, the Holy Void, my true source.

INTENT

It is my intention in writing and sharing this very vulnerable, personal story that it might reach those who have suffered at the hands of any sort of violation and tragedy. It is also for anyone who might feel challenged or overwhelmed by some life circumstance or who simply wishes to take this journey with me of inspiration and miraculous resilience to be reminded of some spark within. May the sharing of my story help you to understand yourself, and your experiences more deeply. May this story encourage you on how to heal. Most of all, know that you have a profound innate healing capacity to rise above anything, to transmute the most horrific acts of darkness, and to reclaim what is your essentialness and awaken from the Dream.

THE INVITATION

I am no different than you. I am a spirit incorporating this vessel of my body, a spark of God, just like all things living in this universe. I am here on a mission just like you, to have experiences, and fulfill this destiny of light dancing in form in my uniqueness, as you are in yours.

I have found everyone to have a unique vibrational signature. It is my experience that everyone has a different soul blueprint of tasks, challenges, gifts, soul contracts, and thus a unique destiny. And yet it has been revealed to me that we are all made of the same cloth, God seeing God. This is just one story. My intention in writing this is to speak out for those who may not have a voice yet, feel safe to speak, or may be silenced. For some, it can mean death and more abuse and pain to speak out. This is also for those who may have forgotten that they can be whatever they wish to be, no matter what has come before, no matter how broken they may have become. Truly anything is possible.

This book is for inspiration of the miraculous resilience of the human spirit, to be reminded of what is possible and mostly of who you really are, Spirit in form.

Perhaps even by the simple act of writing, energy may be freed to ripple out to the many to encourage the throat chakra (energy center) of the world to speak and live in more truth. We are connected in the quantum field of the One. Energy in the form of intention and words flow out and affect the whole.

So, I choose today to do what I could not back then, to simply speak and tell my story of a simple, ordinary woman raised in the deep South who lived through severe trauma later to be re-born and awaken into my true self, the making of a healer.

This book is for all those suffering across the planet in any kind of slavery, torture, or abuse. May these threads of light reach you in your greatest hour of despair and lift you in the love and light that you are. May you know, no matter what, that you have an opportunity to turn poison into gold, and most of all may you know that you're not alone and infinitely, forever supported and loved.

As you breathe, I invite you to reach out from within yourself and know that you are connected to millions, countless other beings, whether known or unknown, who care about your well-being. You may feel the spark of divinity arises within you no matter how dark the suffering is. There is a Light that burns in you. Let that spark light a fire in your heart that will never go out. May the grace of this benevolent source keep you alight and burning beyond even your own ability, capacity, or understanding. And may you receive inherent support from the One whom you are inseparable.

Most of all may the Peace that passes all understanding be with you always.

In Infinity, Isa Lara Marie'

It Acts Like Love

It acts like love – music, it reaches towards the face, touches it, and tries to let you know His promise that all will be okay.

It acts like Love – music and tells the feet, "You do not have to be so burdened."

My body is covered with wounds this world made,

But I still want to kiss Him, even when God said, "Could you also kiss the hand that caused each scar, for you will not find me until you do. It does that – music – helps us to forgive.

— RABIA

HOW BECOMING A SHAMAN HAS BEEN BOTH A BURDEN AND A BLESSING

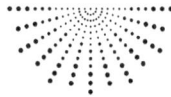

That long, winding silver cord that stretched from the heavens down to me had roots in me like a redwood tree. It felt firm and taught, and sometimes as if that distance was much shorter than from Heaven to here. If I strayed for even a moment from the truth of my guidance, I would feel the inner tug pulling at me like a reminder of something far away but true. At first, I could only feel it, but later in my life, I began to actually see that shimmering silver cord through my psychic vision, and I thought that must certainly be my stairway to Heaven.

The tether of that silver cord was short and made me feel uneasy. It felt like a cord attaching me to my higher or vast self. I came to know this feeling long ago. It did not feel punitive but more like a loving parent, guiding me to stay on the correct path. I call this guidance: "Source." This guiding voice is the one that told me to write this story. Source acts like "love."

Sitting down with my journal in hand, I tried to start writing this story many times, never thinking that I would make it public in the beginning, but simply feeling that the words just wanted to come out on paper and exit my flesh and bones to be released from that cage to flow free. That, perhaps, even in the writing of it, something poetic, some kind of medicine might come forth to soothe the jaggedness of these words. But to no avail, some wall would rise up in me with great resistance, and if I tried to keep going, it would feel like the wall was becoming unscalable. Until one fine day, I was sitting in a workshop on the healing and ending of sexual trafficking and a fire began to rise in my belly. It felt as if my blood lit up with fire and my body began shaking. So, I did what I usually did when something got intense. I closed my eyes, went within, and entered into a deep meditation.

In the faint drone of the lecturer, and the hundreds of people all around me, their sounds drifted further away as I centered myself. I connected with Source and asked: "What can I do to help? What would you like from me?" This bold, yet whispering voice began to repeat: "Write your story, write your story."

This tender, yet whispering voice kept repeating the message until it appeared I understood. I asked for confirmation: "Are you sure?" I reflected on so many things I could do like travel around the world, educate people through speaking, and working with nonprofit organizations. I was hesitant. I did not see how writing my story could be enough. I resisted. The last thing I wanted to do was to share with the world my personal life and the trauma I endured as a child.

I did not want to recall all the events that happened to me and to write them down. I was concerned that, by writing them down, it would give the events more power. I did not want to re-live the events either. I had also been trained in spirituality to not get caught in the story and to remember that we are not "the story." I struggled with the request from Source.

I went through many stages of resistance while saying "yes" if this is what is being asked of me. I am a deeply private and introverted person, so writing a book was certainly not at the top of my list. Yet, I also acknowledged the incredibly powerful platform of storytelling and oral tradition that has helped our species evolve and how learning occurs through this path.

I also know what I endured as a child. I feared sharing my story would re-enliven those experiences and I would feel too much pain. I was also afraid that my family would never speak to me again, even though I knew I would write my story without blame and only through the lens of my lived experiences.

Even though I was hesitant, I decided to write this book. Source has always been a loving and benevolent guide in my life. However, in the spirit of transparency, writing this book has been one of the most difficult things I have experienced in my life. I endured physical pain, emotional pain, and spiritual pain. I had to re-live moments in my life that took me decades to process, unravel, emerge from, and orient. I looked at my life through a telescope and a microscope. I felt anxiety, depression, trauma, humiliation, fear, and shame. I want to share all of this with you now, so you understand the pressure that was relentless to share this message with the world. This is when I realized this story must be told and I was privileged to tell it, simply because I can.

Some people have endured immense trauma, and they are simply unable to share their stories. Others may not have resources, support, or a platform to share their messages. For many others, it may be frightening, too dangerous, or perhaps life-threatening. This is when I realized it was my responsibility and my gift to the world to be able to share this message.

Now I speak for you, your family member, your friend, or anyone you may know who has ever been touched by an unwanted hand or has gone through some challenges in life that feel like too much.

This is not a book solely for sexual abuse survivors, but for anyone wishing to be inspired, and to remember the courage and the resilience of the human spirit amidst formidable conditions.

I am proof that it is possible not only to heal from what feels like unspeakable trauma, but to thrive.

May these words be a beacon of light to guide the opening for truth to emerge in all places, and for acts of abuse, torture, and slavery to cease on this planet.

May these words also be a reminder of the greatness that is possible in any difficult circumstance.

I WRITE THIS FOR YOU.

> Out of suffering have emerged the strongest souls; the most massive characters are seared with scars."
>
> — KHALIL GIBRAN

MY PATH AS A SHAMAN: MY LIFE EXPERIENCE SERVED AS MY TRAINING

In the path of a shaman is often romanticized. But it is not something anyone would normally choose if they knew what it entailed. It is a path with burden and challenge, sometimes to the point of breaking. I experienced many near-death moments, and I had to rise beyond them. Many shamans share similar experiences. They do this for the greater good, not for themselves necessarily, but for others, for the Earth, and for whomever they are helping transmute energy at the time.

First, shamans must learn how to rise above near-death experiences for themselves. They must learn to transform the moment of death into life. Often many people who are called to this path have deep, dark challenges for extended times, very young, and throughout life.

Being a shaman is not special, or better, nor a punishment. I simply see it as a function of what my being came to fulfill in this lifetime. If anyone had said to me in my early years: "You're going to go through all these horrific events, very young for many years, and that is going to end up being your greatest shamanic training" I would have probably said: "No thank you. I do not want that responsibility or that challenge." Like anyone I wanted to enjoy life, feel loved, and comfortable.

MY FORMATIVE YEARS SERVED AS MY EARLY TRAINING TO BECOME A HEALER: I HAVE FEW MEMORIES OF MY VERY EARLY YEARS AS A CHILD

I was born "thick" with Grace, (which is Appalachian southern for "blessed" by grace). Otherwise, I would not be here, sane, and intact to write this now. This grace is not of my doing nor of my will. I cannot take credit for it. Grace is a mysterious force, unexplainable, like a cloud of white fluffy soft light buffering and cushioning you and caring for you just when you need it most and life seems impossible.

I was born six weeks early, premature, from the doctor inducing my mother's labor. This required the doctors to force my tiny head out of my mother's uterus, with cold metal talons they call forceps. Since this was more than half a century ago, I was delivered to a tiny box, with bright lights, and devoid of human touch. This would be a difficult entry for any newborn and for me, it began the early imprint of isolation seen later throughout so much of my life.

We know now, of course, through research, that human contact and bonding are essential in the early moments after birth. In fact, the human brain is 100 billion brain cells that connect to over 7000 other brain cells, making this stage of human development the most significant in a person's life (at times I will be sharing important information as a "gift" to my reader, but for ease of also telling my story, I will not burden you with all of it in the middle of my story. Instead, I will expand on it in an appendix at the end.)

MY FIRST MEMORIES AS A CHILD PROVIDED CLUES OF DYSFUNCTION

I have very few memories of my childhood. People are always asking me questions about what I was like as a child: "Did you eat a certain candy or play a certain game?" I honestly cannot remember many early details. This, I attribute to the chronic childhood emotional and sexual abuse I suffered.

What I do remember is that I had all the appropriate clothes I needed and even new clothes sometimes. We were your average lower middle-class family. I had enough food to eat, water to drink, and a house in which to live.

I grew up on the usual delicious southern poisons of white sugar and white flour. I found out later I was allergic to most of the foods I ate. My parents took me to school. I attended extracurricular activities and even took piano lessons. My Grandmother was set on me learning to play the piano, so Bach, Mozart, Beethoven, and Tchaikovsky came pouring out of my fingertips. I was quite good at playing the piano. I am not sure now whether I really ever enjoyed it. It just felt like something I had to do to please my family. I did enjoy Beethoven and his pieces; all the minor keys were sad and melancholy. At the time, I could relate to that state, and it reached something deep inside of me. It was like the beginning of a place where I could express my sadness without really showing it.

I played basketball because my father wanted me to, and I hated it. I felt nervous and shy and exposed on the court. I was being judged. My father was an extreme perfectionist when it came to these activities. He would push me hard and praise me little. I remember an episode of falling down on the court in the middle of a game. There were a lot of people cheering and watching. I remember the roar of the crowd.

I had turned my ankle. A fog then descended upon me of shame, as if I had done something terribly wrong and failed. It was paralyzing.

I could not get up. Even though I had only slightly turned my ankle, I let them take me out of the game. I was so relieved that I did not have to continue playing. I wanted to disappear. My father was extremely upset with me. He felt I could have pushed through my injury. I failed again. To him, nothing was ever good enough.

Everything in my family looked good to outsiders. My parents did all the normal physical care and activities that one would do for children. Yet, it never felt good being there, like something profound was missing.

MUCH OF WHAT I HAVE COME TO LEARN ABOUT MY EARLY YEARS CAME FROM MY MOTHER

Much of what I have come to learn about my childhood came from my mother.

My mother said when I was little, I would wake up in my crib every night with my hands on the railing, flash the biggest smile, and say: "Hey." All I wanted to do was play.

I am sure that was not very much fun for my parents in the middle of the night. But my mother always reported how I was a happy baby and child. She did share with me one experience of a severe sickness that happened before I turned a year old. Apparently, I had severe colic. After having tried every possible remedy to no avail, they decided to take me to the ocean and left the door cracked open for me to hear the ocean waves. They were shocked and relieved the story goes that I slept then for the first time through the night. This appeared to resolve my sleeping issues and began my eternal love of the ocean. As a child, I always wanted to be near water, especially moving water.

I was also told that once I could walk, I hardly walked at all, but went straight to running. I ran everywhere. I did not want to be helped. I was independent and wanted to do it on my own. I wanted to explore and create. I became irritated when my mother or father would intervene, try to stop me, or help me. I wanted to figure it out for myself.

According to my mother, she always picked me up and never let me crawl. My mother was germophobic and was afraid I was going to pick up germs. She apologized to me as an adult because she learned it was crucial for full neurological development. She was also concerned about the impact it may have had on me when she later learned about my chronic spinal problems.

I was also a very shy child. I remember hiding behind my mother's legs, standing behind her, watching as strangers would greet us. She said I was her gauge for whether people were of good character or not. She would look at me for my reaction. She said I would come out if they were friendly and a good person. If they were anything else, I would cower, hide, and sometimes run off.

I was very affectionate as a child. I remember reaching out to my parents often. I have memories of climbing onto my father's lap, or beside him in the car and curling his hair in my tiny hands. This was a comforting thing that calmed me and brought soothing.

MY PROTECTION OF MY LITTLE BROTHER

When I was four years old, my little brother was born. My mother shared with me that from that first moment, I acted like his little mother. I would carry him everywhere, cradle him, and take care of him, even though I was tiny myself. I loved him and felt as if I was his protector.

My brother and I spent a lot of time playing together in little fantasy creations of worlds that we would make out of odd items, wood and natural blocks, Legos, or whatever was nearby. Like so many children we loved to make forts out of blankets and furniture. We would hide inside the forts and pretend that we were in some far-off world having another life.

I felt extremely protective of my brother, but especially from my mother. I did not want her to act out on or hurt him in any way, and I would often stand up for him and take the punishment from my mother. I worried about him a lot. He felt vulnerable to me as he did not speak until after he was almost four years old. My parents thought something was wrong with him and took him to our local doctor. I was the only one who could understand him. I served as his translator until he could speak so that people could understand him. Somehow, I knew what he wanted, how he felt, and what was going on with him. I would communicate his needs to others. He started to speak after I left for school.

I cannot pinpoint an exact time, but at some point, my brother and I started fighting a lot. At this point in my life, my parents were also at odds with each other and there was a lot of tension in the house. My brother and I would get into violent fights. It was a horrible out-of-control feeling. I know now that we were channeling the anger from my parents. Back then I always wondered what we were really fighting about. All I knew was I was filled with a horrible rage feeling of injustice and feeling blamed for things that I had not done. I wonder now what my little brother was feeling back then.

AS I WAS WRITING MY STORY I EFFORTED TO REMEMBER WHAT I LOVED ABOUT MY CHILDHOOD: BEING OUTDOORS WAS MY SANCTUARY

Trees of every size and variety, that family of green fullness reaching out sprawling above and beyond me, shiny green grass, dirt, and open sky were my refuge. I loved the smell and the feeling of the fresh air on my face and the aliveness I felt when I walked outside, sunlight on my skin. It was my refuge and sanctuary. I wanted to be outdoors, in the thick, humid, wet forest of North Carolina running through the woods and exploring nature and all the little animals everywhere.

We lived in that thick feeling of humidity, like walking through a wet cloud surrounded by a variety of deciduous and evergreens and rich full ground covering. I loved to be outside on new adventures and explorations running through those lands. I was always getting into the dirt. I was often covered from head to toe in what others might refer to as "filth." But to me, it was wonderful. When I would come home, my mother was amazed at how I could tolerate it. She informed me that my brother was fearful of getting dirty. Even so, I always came home with dirt all over me and a smile from cheek to cheek.

I had a treehouse on stilts in my backyard near a big open field with the forest behind it where I could see for miles. I would watch the big sky birds fly over me, usually hawks. They were my mother's favorite bird. Crows and ravens would cackle lining up on the powerlines. I loved watching their interplay. I had little windows in my treehouse where I would live in fantasy worlds for hours with my dolls, toys, and creations of all sorts. I would play for hours and hours until I could hear my mother calling me several times after it got dark. Eventually, I would arrive reluctantly at the back sliding door wishing I did not have to go indoors. I did not want to be inside that cage where the air was not invigorating but instead slowly drained my luster. Entering my house was like entering a wall of tension; palpable, scary, and intimidating.

ANIMALS WERE MY SAVIORS: MY RELATIONSHIP WITH MY BEST FRIEND SANDY

My saving grace showed up as a four-legged half-German Shepherd, half-Collie dog named "Sandy" who was my best friend when I was young. She followed me everywhere, wild and free. She was never on a leash because we lived in a country area, surrounded by woods and hills. She was very protective of me and my family. But she was truly my sidekick. I would romp with her through the woods and run up the dirt road to my neighbor's house to play. We would play on that very long dirt road with our go-karts, motorcycles, bicycles, and skateboards. She ran alongside us.

Sandy would chase me all day long and follow me no matter how tired and exhausted she became. We would snuggle at the end of the day and often spend long periods of time in the outside storage room piled high with boxes. This is a place where I felt safe and at peace. It had a concrete floor and was often cold in the winter, and it served as a haven in the summer in the immense heat of North Carolina. Of course, in a storage room like that, I had to be careful and watch for snakes. We often had copperheads, which are highly poisonous snakes. They would hide in tight areas in our attic, storage areas, yard, and the woods.

I had a close encounter with a copperhead when I was about four years old. An adult-size copperhead had slithered under my legs. I did not have any awareness of the danger. I was marveling at its beauty and enjoying the experience when my mother screamed for me to get up. I am glad she screamed. But from that moment on, I was terrified of snakes. This was obviously a normal reaction of my mother and also a testament to the curiosity and innocence of children.

Sandy and I had many adventures until my early teenage years when she got hit by a car. She was always compelled to chase cars. I never understood why my parents did not get her trained. It never even occurred to me as a child that this was even an option. Animals were kind of wild where we were, at least the ones we had. No one talked about training them. We just let them behave as they were.

When Sandy died, a part of me died too. My heart was broken. She was my best friend in the world. The grief was so immense that I felt it had swallowed me. I did not have anywhere to go for comfort. I longed for my parents to tell me it was going to be all right, to hold me in their loving arms, care for me, and nourish me. I thought they could maybe rub my brow and the wet hair off my face. No solace came. Only extreme stoicism. I needed to be tough, and feelings were not allowed. I needed to be strong and numb to be accepted by my family. No one ever knew my deepest sadness and experience of the loss of my best friend. I was alone fending for myself.

> Goodbyes are only for those who love with their eyes; for those who love with heart and soul there is no separation."
>
> — RUMI

MY FASCINATION AND LOVE OF HORSES SHOWED ME THEIR POWER AND GRACE

From the tiniest age as soon as I could speak, I was in love with horses. My parents said it was all I talked about. I asked for one every year. Fortunately, my mother had a horse at my cousin's house about half an hour away, but she was a bit wild. We did not get to ride her often as she was not as tame as the kind of horse that would be safe for me to ride regularly. She was a bit of a handful. My favorite times were when my mother would let me ride her bareback and lead me around. This seemed to be safe enough, and she would stay calm with someone leading her slowly. My little legs could not quite reach down far enough for a saddle and my arms were shy of holding the reins. I was in love with her black and white puzzle-looking coat slathered on a furry, sleek body. She was an Appaloosa and had beautiful white and black spots. I thought she was the most beautiful thing I had ever seen.

There were other horses boarded at my cousin's ranch. I loved to watch them and sense their power, freedom, and grace. I loved when they would suddenly start neighing, running, playing, and kicking. It would send a surge of energy through my body and a tingling feeling. It made me feel alive. I wanted to join them, and I would run alongside the fence following them as far as my little legs could go, feeling free with our wild spirits joined.

Finally, in my teens, my partial dream came true. I was able to find a job at several different horse stables near my home where I could work and ride horses whenever I wished. I spent every free moment outside of school working at these ranches, riding horses on trails, and exercising them in the arenas.

MUSIC BECAME A REFUGE FOR ME AND THE ONLY CONNECTION WITH MY FATHER

Music moved me so deeply and on the notes of the melody I would get a glimpse of other worlds. It was also one of the ways I remember I could connect with my father. My father lived and breathed music. He could name every artist from his time and how they moved his soul. He could describe the poetic lyrics underlying their music. I could sense a deep, emotional state while he was listening to his music, which I never sensed of him otherwise and his heart would shine through for a moment only to tuck back in hiding after the music stopped.

This always perplexed me, because I did not understand how my father had such sensitivity regarding music and yet showed little or no emotions in life. He would explain to me endlessly about the artist and their stories, and from where their songs derived. Immediate pictures would rise up in my mind with color and grandeur about these artists, and their soulful lives. Then he would turn the music on at its highest volume, sing loudly, and look at me with big, sad eyes. He seemed to be checking in with me to ensure I was hearing the story that was being told and understanding it. He was moved and touched by this, and he wanted me to know it. I think I was the main person in the family that could connect with him in this place. Everyone else seemed to observe him from a distance when he was lost in his music. But I would enter his world. At least I could find him for a moment in a lyric of a song or a loud beat.

My father would work all day at a job he hated carrying the burden of his father's company. Then, in the evening, drinking, exhausted, and in another world, he would float on the notes of the music. Sometimes, when I was lucky, we would take a drive in the car. It did not matter what time of year either. We would roll the windows down, feel the blast of cold air on our cheeks, blow the heat on our feet, and blast the music on high. This was one of my favorite times with my father because I could feel he was happy. Rarely did I ever feel my father was happy. I also felt that it was a way that I could connect to him, even though he seemed mostly untouchable. I learned back then to appreciate the depth and gift of music. To this day it is one of my greatest joys in life.

> It acts like love—music, it reaches toward the face, touches it, and tries to let you know.
>
> His promise: that all will be okay."

— RABIA

OUR FAMILY ENVIRONMENT WAS FRAGMENTED GROWING UP: I LIVED IN FEAR OF MY MOTHER

Fear and rage consumed my mother daily when I was a child. I walked on eggshells continuously.

I learned later this was a result of her unhealed process from her childhood trauma. She carried copious pharmaceuticals in her purse out of fear of needing them but was too scared to take them. Even as a child, I felt so much empathy for her and I just wanted her to feel okay. But my mother never seemed to be calm or at peace. What I remember most were her cold clammy hands, and how as they touched me, they always told me that something was wrong and that the world was not safe. Her hugs were like chilling ice, stiff, and distant. I longed to be held and told that everything would be okay, for her to wrap her arms around me with warmth and comfort me, but that did not come.

In my mother's fits of rage, she would fly off the handle over nothing and she would beat me. She would then feel guilty and come to me immediately calling me her "Angel," holding me suffocatingly tight and crying over me while apologizing. She did something called "Switching." She would switch from one personality to another very quickly and you never knew who was going to show up. I later called this the "Jekyll and Hyde" syndrome. I am not claiming that my mother was mentally ill because this was through my eyes as a child and my experience. Yet, when she switched so quickly and erratically to hold me tight after raging at me, her hugs were suffocating and frightening. Her hugs were not reassuring. In fact, I would shake and wall myself off to stay safe deep inside myself. In that way, I told myself, that as a child, she could not reach me, and this is how I developed my coping skills to feel safe.

This is how I first learned, as a child, to not let anything in and to protect myself. I learned it first with my mother before the religious cult abuse reinforced this.

In one of my mother's episodes in my youth, we were in my room disagreeing about something, which was not allowed in my family. She took her arm wildly flailing it towards me and cleared everything off my desk by slinging it towards me. One of the items was a sharp good-sized picture frame. It came by with such force that it made a hole in the wall behind my head. All I could think was that if that had hit me, I would be severely injured.

I was terrified of my mother my whole life. I even thought she was going to kill me at times. I felt that she wanted to sometimes. The rage that kept emerging from her regularly over the smallest things from just asking a question or having a different opinion, or disagreeing about something would send her from 0 to 100 on the rage scale within seconds. It was not that she hit me all the time. In fact, it was not even daily. Her behavior was simply unpredictable. Her rage would rise up, and she would come at me quickly, even physically sometimes chasing me. I would run from her into my room, close the door, lock it, hide in my closet, and wait for her screaming, and beating on the door to stop. There are so many episodes of her raging that float through my mind. I simply cannot remember what happened afterward. It was like I left my body and blanked out.

I have many empty spaces of not knowing and being able to remember what happened to me in my childhood. Mostly what I get are snippets like a puzzle you are putting back together but not in an organized linear fashion. Instead, it is jumbled and chaotic, like a radio station that just will not come in clearly. Unfortunately, the very nature of being unable to lay memories down after trauma can make victims doubt their memories later, especially when they have been fractured.

Many of my mother's fits would center around her obsessive-compulsive disorder too. Sometimes, I would not place something in its correct position or do it properly according to her standards. When things like this happened, instead of speaking to me calmly and communicating her preferences, there would be another angry outburst.

Another regular practice of my mother's that I also noticed was that she would blame me for something that I had not done or for the acts of my siblings. This would happen regularly and automatically. I would share what really happened and try to explain myself. But she did not listen to me. She assumed it was my fault, and that I was the family scapegoat. Then I would wait as she threatened that my father would be home and belting me at the end of the day. Or if she lost control sooner, she would chase me with the belt and get me at some point. I was constantly being punished for acts that I did not commit. In some ways, I was glad that I could spare the punishment for my brother. Yet as I got older that got harder to tolerate.

I ached for my father to be there, to guide me and comfort me. I wanted him to tell me that everything was going to be all right. I desperately wanted him to feel pleased about who I was and express it to me. I longed for his strength and guidance. But it never came. I felt deeply abandoned by him. I retreated into my inner world with my animals and nature.

I FELT ABANDONED BY MY FATHER

My father was passive, controlling, and fearful. He worked in the days and when he was around, he was not really there, because he was passed out drunk. He would retreat to his world of music with the headphones blasting and my little hands would reach for the clasps pulling them down off his head to see if I could find him in there. I would slide them down and call his name, but my father had gone into his own world, far away from me.

I was left alone with the coldness of absence and had to fend for myself with my mother. She would regularly report to him when he got home that he needed to belt me, and he would robotically do the job. I could never tell if he wanted to or not and I even glimpsed that, at times, he may have felt guilty. But he did not dare stand up to my mother, who would regularly distort happenings, blaming and shaming me while I anxiously awaited my father to return home from work to belt me.

I do not remember as much about my father because he was mostly gone and therefore, I spent much less time with him except for the lucky musical car rides. I do remember he talked incessantly without a pause, and if he asked a question, would give me just a couple of seconds to respond and then interrupt me again and continue talking. I found this exhausting. He abhorred silence and could never allow that in a conversation or moment. The space needed to be filled and I could feel how uncomfortable he was inside his own skin. Eventually, I stopped listening and would just zone out to get a break.

I stopped trying to speak because I was only able to get in a few words at a time without being interrupted. It just did not make any sense to even try to speak after a while. I was just like a robot, following rules and orders. I did what he wanted me to do, and eventually became a conduit to fulfill his unmet dreams. I was given a very firm message that I was there to fulfill what he wanted, his dreams, his ideas of reality, and how life was supposed to be, and that I needed to do that right down to even going to the only school that he agreed to pay for and let me attend. Yet, I really appreciated that support as some do not even get that in their lives.

MY GRANDPARENTS WERE PREDOMINANT FORCES IN OUR LIVES AND THEIR IMPRINTS WERE SEVERE

My grandparents on both sides wielded considerable influence in our lives, whether they were around us physically or not. Their imprints on my parents as young children, and even as adults, had an enormous impact on us growing up.

I saw how my father's parents started to become a predominant force in our lives. They had very strong and bold personalities. They were also extremely religious. We spent a lot of our time with them, and considerably more than with my mother's family.

My father seemed to be controlled by his father. He did what his father wanted, and lived to uphold whatever values, beliefs, or wishes that his father had, even if he did not feel in alignment with them. It was hard to watch my father suffer, especially when he hated his job in the company, working for my grandfather.

My grandfather was the son of a preacher, and he would speak of the scripture, what was right and wrong, and how it was important to do the work of the Bible. He had very strong ideas about what was allowed and what was not allowed and if you did not fit into that belief system, it was clear that you were going to go to hell.

While I did not want to go to hell, I knew all the things he was saying really did not land with me. Sometimes I tried to argue with him, but I would get in trouble and end up being punished and shut down. What was made most clear was that I needed to do what my grandparents ordered. It did not matter what I thought or felt. I was not allowed to express myself or my beliefs. I just needed to regurgitate what I was told, stay in line, and act the part. I found that hard to do even though I tried my best. It made me feel sick to my stomach. My Grandparents on both sides were extremely devout and being saved by Jesus and not sinning was burnt into my skin through scary words and threats.

It was not a surprise we spent most of our time with my father's side of the family. My mother was estranged from her family and had limited contact. Her father was shut down and did not speak much at all. I always felt scared being around him. He exuded a feeling of deep, dark repressed secrets that were so tightly wound I thought one day that knot might burst. I did not want to be there when that explosion happened. My maternal grandmother was an alcoholic and treated my mother poorly. She always favored her other daughter. This caused my mother great pain and she often spoke about it with bitterness. I felt sorry for my mother. I wanted her to feel the love of her mother. In turn, I longed to feel my mother's love and her warmth towards me. But that never came.

MY PARENTS NEVER GIFTED ME MY OWN EXISTENCE: I LIVED FOR THEM

With both my parents, the theme was that I did not have a separate existence. I was there to fulfill their reality of who they were supposed to be, but could not become, their unfulfilled dreams, and perhaps even some sort of legacy. I was not allowed to be a separate being. I remember asking my mother several times in my youth if she would knock on my door before coming in when my door was closed. She did not allow me to ask for privacy. In fact, she began to yell and rage at me and bust through time after time, telling me that that was not acceptable.

I was not allowed boundaries and I was not allowed to be separate from my mother in any way. This is how I began to lose myself for a very long time. I was given the message that I did not matter and that I was there to serve others and let others do whatever they wanted, and that I could not have boundaries. I was given a very strong message that I needed to please people no matter what, and just allow them to act towards me however they wanted without speaking out. Every year growing up, I shrunk more and became invisible. I was told to not really be in myself, or occupy my own space, or that I even had a right to be myself. All this conditioning made me highly susceptible to perpetrators when I encountered them.

I observed how disconnected my parents were and how they fought daily. When they were not fighting, they were estranged like they really did not understand each other, much less have a good or peaceful connection. This caused me to become a family caregiver. I was already the most organized and diligent. But this is not a role you want to assume as a child. Even so, I would wake everyone up in the morning to ensure they were on time for whatever task they needed to accomplish. I would also serve as a counselor and support for my parents, which often involved deeply disturbing conversations that were highly inappropriate for a child of my age. I became more like a confidante, a friend, or even a parent. The roles were completely reversed. This often made me sad. I had no one to turn to for support for myself, my challenges, or my needs. I felt deeply lonely.

At age 14 my parents finally decided to separate and my mother's distance, animosity, and brutality towards me increased even more. She also exhibited jealousy towards me regarding my father. She wanted all the attention so if I was connecting with my father in any way, she would become upset and ensure she was the focus. She wanted my attention and for me not to be too close to my father. At this point, however, I had come more into my power and was tired of putting up with her tyrannical rages which were quite unpredictable. This was the beginning of a lifelong estrangement for us. At age 16 I finally left her house to live with my father. This was a welcome transition, yet I left one challenge and went to another.

Their separation, even though it appeared obvious and needed to happen, created its own challenges. Naturally, as a child I wanted my parents to be together. It was shocking and destabilizing. My father coped with it by making me his surrogate wife. He treated me as if I was an adult, emotionally, and confided in me by telling me things about himself and relying on me in ways that were inappropriate for a child/parent relationship. My father and I were in an entanglement.

His emotional need and dependence on me were intense. I worried for his well-being. I felt guilty when I was going to leave for college and I was not sure if he was going to be stable enough, especially with his level of drinking.

In my childhood, and upon reflection, I came to learn, that my parents focused on themselves, and not our needs as children. They behaved like lost children themselves and often I was the parent, or at least I made attempts to parent, even though I was too little.

During this time, I was continually being taught the Bible and about sin. The doctrines were heavy, and one had to abide by them, or you would be ostracized. I had no idea what I really felt being that young. Jesus and Mary seemed like good people but what was happening to me at the church, was the opposite of good.

OUR CHURCH SERVED AS A SECOND PRIMARY HOME

From as far back as I can remember, I had a burning love for God or Source. Early on I called it, God, the all-pervading great mystery of a power from where we come, and what sustains us. I used to pray all the time. I would sing my little heart out in church, happy to praise through holy ancient hymns that seemed from some other place. It made me happy and felt true.

While I was growing up, our church was like my second home. I came from a long line of extreme religiosity as part of a preacher's family. Religion was ingrained in both sides of my family. We attended the big church on the hill in the country every week. It was about a 20-minute drive from our home. I did not really like that long drive. I always had the strangest feeling in the pit of my stomach, like I was being taken somewhere I really did not want to go. It felt like a completely other world, far and removed.

My father's cousins and extended family attended the same church. I would get a creepy feeling when I would see some of my male cousins. One of them made deeply inappropriate comments to me about my body. He sexualized and objectified me and made rude comments. I feared him. I wanted him to stay away from me. But Sunday after Sunday, my family convened. I was expected to be a good girl and interact appropriately.

The church was enormous with very high ceilings and stained-glass windows. I always felt I was going to be lost in there, and engulfed by some presence. I felt watched by these high saints etched into the stained-glass windows and grand statues. I had a feeling of losing my parents there because we attended often. It felt big. I would be in a different place.

We also had catechism, sometimes Bible school, camps in the summer, and what they called pot pie gatherings in the south. They held those in the parish hall building. I hated that building. I did not know why back then, but I always felt trapped like I could not breathe. I just wanted to get out.

There was a kitchen with closed doors. Next to it was a big open room with two separate rooms and some small bathrooms in between. There was a strange tiny outbuilding. I do not remember what was in there, but it was very small and tight. It was a strange room that seemed to have no purpose. To the side of this outbuilding was a huge hill, with rolling, sprawling green acreage. On the other side, there were huge basketball courts with a vast paved parking area. It was as if they were expecting hundreds of people and back then at times we did have that kind of church population.

There was one particular church bathroom I did not like going into because it felt like ice. I had a chilling fear upon entering. I always thought it was strange that the door could be locked because it was one of those bathrooms with a public stall inside and a closed door, yet the main door could be locked.

The main vestibule, upon entering, was very formal. I always felt self-conscious and intimidated wondering if judgment was going to come down on me.

The Church held Sunday school in a separate building. You had to walk down narrow steps and enter a basement. It was a big area with a lot of classrooms. It had tables and chairs and a tiny window with faint light. When I went down the basement stairs, I would get an uneasy feeling in my stomach and sometimes in my spine. I liked this building the least. It felt secluded. It had little light. It was dank, dark, and musty. This is where we spent our time during Sunday school and catechism, and sometimes summer camps, and other activities. We also spent time here during Bible study nights when we would have to move to different spaces within the church premises.

My family found it unacceptable to miss any Church activities, especially a Sunday morning service. My parents seemed very anxious about anything having to do with Church and were vigilant about our attendance in all activities. We also felt family pressure from our grandparents. My father was shamed by his father if we missed Church for any reason.

After Sunday Church activities were over, we went to my great-grandmother's house for a huge family lunch. It was like a scene out of a movie. Everyone attended: all my cousins, grandparents, aunts, and uncles - there were about 20 of us at a time. My great-grandmother on my father's side was the head of this matriarchy. She was a tough, stoic one. Her motto was work and silence. While we visited, the older women in the family prepared the feast which consisted of enormous southern style displays of food on the tables. I welcomed this part of my Sundays. Nourishment was delivered through this elaborate display of food. This felt like the main way the women in the family felt loved and appreciated. It was through their cooking and nourishing all of us. They kept delivering food to all of us and it was hard for us to turn it down as they kept saying with a southern smile: "Oh, you're too thin, have some more." I think deep down, even back then, I also felt this might have been a way they may have also felt appreciated and loved.

My great-grandmother's demeanor was very rigid and cool. She did not exhibit much warmth, gentleness, or openness. Her love came through her food and nourishment. After Sunday lunch was over, the cousins would go outside to the big field and play football or baseball. Since I was athletic and loved the outdoors, I would play with them. I enjoyed moving my body intensely. These were some of the few good memories I can recall.

Going outside after Sunday Church became an escape where I could lose myself amidst my troubles, our lack of true family connection, and from what I remembered later was really happening in the hallowed walls of the Church.

MY PARENTS DELIVERED ME TO THE CHURCH CULT WHERE I WAS RITUALLY SEXUALLY ABUSED

It is hard to even say the word "abuse" let alone write it. Moments of abuse are one thing. The aftermath of being abused is a whole other story. When abuse occurs and it "ends," it is only over in the physical world but not in the victims' nervous system, psyche, and body for years to come.

The aftereffects of abuse are paramount, long term, and affect every area of a person's life. When abuse occurs, innocence is destroyed as well as inherent trust in the universe, people, and safety. Scary beliefs about the dangers of the world become a victim's norm.

The intelligent being we are copes in the best way possible at the moment. If the abuse is severe enough, shock may ensue followed by dissociation. When abuse occurs, in the victim's mind, it can feel like an out-of-body experience, as if witnessed from a distance. This becomes a way for the victim to begin coping with being abused. Others may not be so lucky and the core essence may be touched by the abuse and crack. What we call mental illness may then ensue.

For some people reading this, it may be triggering, especially if you have been a victim of sexual abuse. I have done my best to sanitize some of the details so that I can share with you more of the pain and suffering and fewer graphic details. Even so, as I have shared before, my memories are fragmented, as well, due to the suffering I experienced. When you endure a trauma, like mine, at any point in your life, it is difficult to lay down memories in a linear, coherent pattern.

As I child, I did not understand what a cult was or even begin to question what the group wanted or their purpose.

I only began to realize later that the men who engaged in childhood sexual abuse did so because they wanted our innocence as children because we were pure, full of vitality and potency. We were untouched and young. They were the takers who had forgotten who they were, which was part of God.

As a child, what I witnessed was true evil.

When they cornered me, which was often, I would go up and out. This is perhaps where my love and obsession with wings began.

The perpetrators seemed unconcerned that I was going up and out. They were focused and fooled by my body's form. They did not notice it was empty, limp, and distressed. They were seeking massive shock value and intense currents of energy from the adrenaline release which they ingested, harnessed, and thrived off as mad addicts. They were chemically altering themselves in hopes of absolution all "in the name of God," sin, and punishment.

My body was drugged, tied up, hogtied to be exact, twisted in and out of painful positions, used, and violated in every orifice possible right under the steeple and stained glass, as images of Christ and statues of saints also viewed the atrocities. Chanting, hooded, calloused forms haunted the hallways of that supposed sanctuary.

These dark beings entered my body hungry and devouring. We were the easiest victims, being small and not developed yet. The abusers seemed to be looking for their own purity, so they attempted to take ours. They rocked back and forth on their heels in their long-hooded cloaks chanting the name of God and calling forth each child to obey them or else they would be punished. They threatened us with our lives continually.

I was sexually abused for many years during my youth well into my mid-teenage years. The church cult would sexually abuse me, sometimes one solo abuser at a time, forcing me into some unimaginable sexual act for a child. Other times they would gather a small group of children with the perpetrators in a circle and pass children around, one at a time, sexually abusing us. We were forced to watch. We could not leave. We could not help each other. Even screaming was prohibited. They threatened that they would kill my family If I spoke out. They threatened all of us that they would kill our families.

I remember countless episodes of sexual abuse. There are details imprinted in my mind. I remember their robes, some kind of choir and pastoral robes, big looming above and around me. I was pulled, prodded, mangled in different ways, held back, forced to perform oral sex, or having my little body forcefully entered by some huge, enormous monster. Sometimes I was vaginally raped, sometimes anally. Sometimes my face was pressed to the table where I was unable to see or move or to relieve the horrible excruciating pain in my little body. They always told me it was in the name of God and for God and that I had done something bad and therefore I was being punished. This is what they told all of us children, that we were being punished for our sins.

MY CHILDHOOD SEXUAL ABUSE INFILTRATED MY FAMILY CORE

I have another memory of being sexually abused at nine years old in this dark dank basement of my relative's home close to the church.

In this memory, I fixate on the shaggy carpet and the smell of mold and mustiness. It is all I can do is focus as hard as my little mind can on this so that I survive and do not lose my mind or die of fright.

There are no windows. It is very dim lighting as the door is bolted shut. I am trapped. I am a prisoner as the sound of a belt is undoing. As the zipper opens it sends sheer terror and cringing through my little body. This time, I shoot up and out of my body not sure if I am still alive. I hover watching from above.

Two of my male relatives have me in a room, taking their turn with me and raping me. They are members of the church cult. I find myself hovering again, fixating on the awful smells, and the dim lighting and that shag carpet. I feel like if I just keep my attention there then somehow, I might survive. It is as if everything else is shut out. He is jamming his member into my tiny body, and I am choking and feeling suffocated. I cannot breathe. One of them covers my face with a pillow to quiet my whimpering sounds. He is choking me with his hands intermittently as he lifts the pillow, so I have a moment of air, and the back and forth continues. I pass out. (This is a control mechanism from cults to program victims by taking them near death and then letting them live. It shows you that your life is in their hands and that you have no control. The message is: submit or die.)

I am not sure how much time passed or how I was revived. That part is all blank. But I do know that I lost consciousness. This happened many times to me during the sexual abuse episodes. I came to, feeling shock and disorientation and panicked because I did not know where I was nor how to orient myself.

I knew I had to get out.

The next thing I remember was bolting and running out of the room. I exited the room like a wild animal into the backyard. I had to get away so that they did not get me again. This land was in the middle of nowhere, just like the church, and within one mile of it. It was a wild area in the country with a ton of acreage and forests. I ran at full speed, trying to escape. I panicked and suddenly realized that my young childhood friend was behind me chasing me. I had no remembrance of her until this moment of how she got there or from where she came. She had come to visit this place with me. I turned around to call her name and look at her while I ran at full speed through the heavily forested land.

Smack! I ran straight into a barbed wire fence.

It flipped me on my back and underneath the wire. The next thing I remember was people were helping me rise. I was bloody. My mouth was injured. Several of my front teeth were dangling and I had cuts across my stomach. My relatives called my parents and, of course, just reported I was playing in the forest and ran into a fence. My parents arrived and took me to a medical facility where they decided to shove my teeth back up by applying pressure and reported my teeth would be okay. I was given a tetanus shot and no other part of my body was checked for abuse.

I was dazed and confused about how the accident happened. I had been on this land many times. At this point, I had already unconsciously shut out the memory to cope.

Later in the following years, I had to have three root canal surgeries because of this injury in my teeth and gum area. Finally, after the last surgery, I evaluated that it was best to have my injured teeth surgically removed. The pain was not getting any better and the specialist I saw said that the teeth were dead already. He was concerned that I had an infection all these years in my body because of the accident. I then received several extensive surgical procedures to remove my front teeth and create a bridge which the dentist had never done before with the device that would allow balance in my cranial plate and system because it crossed the midline of my body. It had to be done with incredible accuracy and delicacy, so as not to disrupt the balance of my cranial sacral system.

When I underwent the teeth extraction surgery thick pus flowed out my mouth and out of the cavity for many days. I was quite ill. My body was discharging the infection that had been living in my body for over a decade.

As a young adult, I was terrified to have my front teeth removed. The world focuses so much on our image and our face. Imagine having your front teeth removed. I began feeling shame and disgust. I also felt grief and loss. My teeth somehow reminded me of my childhood innocence, and I was just beginning to touch this experience from a long time ago.

Having my front teeth removed created more than emotional and spiritual trauma. I had to learn how to speak again as well. They placed a gold plate in my mouth during the surgery which impinged my palate and impacted my tongue. I could no longer pronounce words the same way. To this day, it still feels uncomfortable and foreign in my mouth. It is not natural.

Before this happened, I began having nightmares of losing my teeth. In my dreams, I would panic. My teeth began falling into my hands. I tried to scream at my parents, but I was unable to make any sounds. They looked at me as if nothing was happening and ignored me in my franticness. This was a repetitive dream. Sometimes they would say "Just come over here" dismissively. I would scream in silence. I was not being heard. This jarred me awake in a cold sweat, shaking. This is a recurring dream I had until about a decade ago. During a psychotherapy session in adulthood, I learned it was about not being heard. I was trying to speak out, but no one was listening. I had been exhibiting signs of terror and of needing help. I was reaching out to my parents for help. My dream demonstrated my feelings of loss, *terror, and grief.*

The worst part for me during the sexual abuse was having to watch other children, and not feeling that I could protect them or rescue them. That was the most excruciating pain and helplessness I have ever felt.

They made us witness the others being tortured and raped. This was part of their enslavery and mind control. I do not know if you have ever watched someone you love being harmed and you could not do anything about it while being forcefully held back or threatened. It was worse watching others being abused than when it happened to me. It was like my heart was being ripped out of my body. I had to watch other children including my familiars being tortured. This haunted me for years and I wanted to die. I would have repetitive dreams where I could not save the children, even though I was one of them. I was also left with survivor's guilt and felt terrible that I had survived and even thrived in my adult life after healing.

This group abuse of many perpetrators abusing a child one after the other and simultaneously in front of the group was a way of enhancing mind control through mass humiliation, exposure, and inducing terror. There is a humiliation and exposure factor that gets created in a more pronounced way when there is group abuse occurring as opposed to individual abuse. The shame that sets in for the victim allows the abusers to control the children more fully, for when you feel you are broken and damaged it is easier to feel you "deserve" what is happening. The feelings of powerlessness and helplessness are overwhelming.

The level of humiliation that I experienced felt intolerable. I felt vulnerable and exposed, like there was nothing inside of me left that had not been taken, used, or discarded. Shame flooded my body like a river for many years, creating the most intense feeling of self-hatred as if it were my fault.

I always wondered why the abusers did not kill me. Believe me, I wanted to die. The perpetrators as they tortured and raped us would constantly take us to the edge of death through horrific acts of violence. They used methods of suffocation mainly through their hands strangling and through pillows and would take me to the point where the breath was gone from my body. Everything would turn black and stop for a moment and I was gone unto this world. Then at the precise moment to save me, they would release the suffocation and the hold on my body, and the breath would return, and I would remain. They used their bare gnarly hands, pillows, and their gross billowy bodies. Everything was a weapon to them.

I realized later that they would not kill me, because that would risk their capture and they wanted ongoing victims to use. I reflected later that perhaps because they were so close to me in weekly physical proximity, which is why they did not kill me. In studies, it is shown that they are more likely to kill the victims if they are strangers. I was no stranger to them. The preacher, ex-Navy Seal, heading the cult, had skills. He knew how to keep secrets. There are many ways of killing. Some are the slow, insidious kind that could kill you over time from the inside out. I was determined not to let that happen.

Many years later I found out that that preacher, the leader of the cult, had been fired from our church because they said he was "insane," even though I suspect they never found out what he was doing, and thus he was never caught.

After coming to from the suffocation, the shock and dissociation then ensued. The numbness and disorientation created so much confusion and listlessness that my body would go limp, apathy would arise, and I would feel completely lost, numb, not unaware of where I was physically. I was disoriented to time and space.

These control tactics also hindered my ability to speak or make any sound. The fight or flight mechanism is repeatedly activated within a victim as chemicals flood the body and terror ensues making all other mental faculties inoperable. Survival is the only thing at hand. I became flooded with only trying to stay alive.

Suffocation was the hardest visceral memory to heal, and I still have it triggered to this day by certain factors. It created the worst feeling of claustrophobia. It took me years to be able to ride in an elevator, fly on a plane, go into public bathrooms, drive on bridges, and for several years even drive alone. The panic would rise so insurmountable that I was trapped in some small space and could not get out. This caused tight squeezing in my chest, a pounding racing pulse, and terror, especially when it seemed there was no exit.

The perpetrators were excited by the extreme violence, control, and the levels of fear that it elicited. I was trapped in bondage often in small spaces, bathrooms, closets within the church, parish hall, Sunday school buildings, and private residences of the cult members.

This was a form of severe and effective mind control that many cults use to program the minds of their victims to ensure access, secrecy, and control. It traps a person's system in a chronic state of amygdala hyperarousal which then sets the autonomic nervous system into total dysregulation.

Hyperarousal of the amygdala is when through repetitive traumas the amygdala gland (which affects our autonomic nervous system and limbic system, memories, etc., and is located in the lower, central part of the brain called the mammalian brain) gets overstimulated and set on high gear. It then begins overreacting, judging many things to be unsafe, which actually are safe. A specific example is this dysregulation can cause chronic allergies across the board.

Also, in these episodes, I would black out and wake up with extreme disorientation. I would not know where I was even in space and feel lost and confused. It felt like if I stayed in my body I would die, and all I wanted to do was just get out.

I do not really know where my parents were during this time. I was a child, and they were dropping me off at the church for all these different activities including Sunday school, Bible study, catechism, and summer camps. There were other times they were at the church doing something else, while I was in these events. The only place I remember them being with me was on Sundays during worship service in the big chapel and at the big southern family lunch afterward.

As I had described, the church grounds were huge covering many acres with fields and rolling green hills surrounding it. There were no neighbors in sight. The whole church compound was elaborate with many different buildings on the land. There were many separate buildings with entrances and exits, separate from the main church. I do not know where the other parents were either. All I remember is the groups of men watching and abusing us. I do not know quite how they organized it or figured it out, but they were an organized group led by the preacher. I knew he was the head because he was the main one always commanding everyone. My father told me later that he was an ex-Navy seal and that they fired him when I was 14 years old. All I knew was that he was insane.

I learned very young the process of annihilation when I finally realized that fighting and resisting were futile. The immenseness of the perpetrators and the weight of their bodies upon me and inside of me sent searing pain shooting up into my womb, pelvis, and sides. I felt shooting pain throughout my pelvis and abdomen as they would take turns raping me one after the other. The stench and sound of their toxic breath filled me with heaving nausea as I wrestled with every cell I had within to throw them off me but to no avail. In the background was the droning sound of cult chanting, and the faint visual of hoods and robes rocking and swaying. I never knew when it was my turn or when they would come for me.

After some time, I was frozen and flying way above and beyond the church's cold cell wall. Sometimes they used their swollen, disgusting penises of fire or their tongues or fingers and, at other times they used random objects shoving them inside of me. Every part of my body would scream in pain as they would pull and flay out my extremities, legs and arms splayed open and tied me down as they inserted themselves or things into my body, especially my vagina, anus, and mouth. Other times they would "hog-tie" me and the other children as more control tactics to show us we could not escape. This made us submissive. My stomach rolled and turned vomiting out their stench until I was delirious with dehydration, terror, and loss.

Then some force completely took me over and I surrendered myself to the torture, pain, and heinousness. I escaped my body. In those times I was able to rise above the abuse and it became only experiences, as if I was a witness to them, and outside my body.

To survive trauma a victim can develop a coping skill to remove themselves from the situation, the point of no return, a sheer exhaustion and breaking down where resistance has become futile, to a form of grace that comes in and helps the person survive what is occurring.

THE IMPACT ON MY LIFE AS A RESULT OF MY CHILDHOOD SEXUAL ABUSE

It is painful to write these words, but as I have vowed to show up vulnerable in this book and to share my story, I would be remiss if I did not share it fully. The darkness was so strong at times I would feel pulled towards death.

If I Had Not Believed

> Would any seed take root if I had not believed His promise, when God said, "Dears, I will rain. I will help you. I will turn into warmth and effulgence. I will be the Mother I am and let you draw from my body and rise and rise."
>
> — ST. THOMAS OF AQUINAS

MY FIRST RESPONSE TO MY CHILDHOOD TRAUMA AND SEXUAL ABUSE WAS AN EFFORT TO CONTROL MY BODY

The trauma began to leak through my journey with anorexia-bulimia. I wanted to disappear. I desperately needed one thing I could control. It seemed as if the only choice in my life was to control what or when to eat, and it had become my dying obsession. My parents commanded my entire reality, what I could do, could not do, and when I could do it. They thrived on controlling feelings and keeping up all appearances of looking like a happy family. The family mantra was: "Don't cry, don't be angry, don't express yourself, just smile all the time no matter what."

But I did not know how to do that while being raped, beaten, and tortured by the perpetrators of the church and their secret society, so slowly inside I faded.

I chose one thing I could control: what I chose to eat. I deprived myself of food. Then I submersed myself in moments of binge eating followed up with excessive marathon-like exercise to focus all my attention on the perfection of my body. This extreme focus called all my attention into a trance-like state where this became my obsession. I felt high. I was flooded with feeling for a moment. I felt better, happier, and free. I look back now and realize that was an endorphin release. I had been experiencing so many negative chemicals that had been flooding my body for so long, this was one of the few places my body could experience a high. I felt as if I had control over this one and only thing in my life. My entire focus kept me from feeling any feelings or memories suppressed inside of me.

I continued like this in hiding as long as I could until I became frail. I began to slowly fade, wandering around almost robot-like, with my spirit elsewhere. I do not know how I existed or lived or even drove a car without crashing it, except once.

I became wispy, iron-deficient, and ceased menstruating. I shrank visibly until finally my parents threatened me with a live-in hospital program. They wanted to place me in an in-patient anorexia program which shocked and broke the trance in which I was living.

I was terrified to be locked in that sterile fluorescent-lit box with shiny floors and white walls of Clorox. Tiny windows squeezed the light narrowing it into tiny shafts of spots leaking on the floors, as if somehow it was not supposed to be there, and it had gotten in. The feelings of suffocation and entrapment squeezed their gnarly, ghostly fingers around my ribs. I folded. I promised to start eating and gaining weight. Even so, they took me on a tour through a hospital unit. The tour through the hospital unit was a nightmare in itself. I remember feeling that eating or not was the last and only thing I could control and now that was going to be taken from me.

No one realized my anorexic/bulimic behavior was really an issue of control and the repercussions of severe abuse. No one looked deeply nor asked any hard questions. I excelled in all things and my family looked good to everyone on the outside. They categorized it as something that "many teenage girls go through," a fad, and that I would grow out of it.

As I exited the hospital doors, I vowed to myself to eat or do anything to keep from being jailed in there. I made it my mission to eat just enough to put on a few pounds, to slow the scare, and to distract everyone from focusing on me. I was screaming on the inside, and no one could hear me. I could not even make a sound, even though my internal scream was eviscerating me.

BEFORE LEAVING FOR UNIVERSITY, I GAINED ENOUGH COURAGE TO ASK MY MOTHER IF I WAS RAPED

Right before I left for university, I gained the courage to enter the kitchen where my mother was and ask her "Mom, have I ever been sexually abused? "I knew it sounded strange as if the words were floating out of bubbles on my mouth and I was far away from them. I knew it was also a weird thing to say, but it rose up and flew out of my mouth. *How could not one person know if I had been raped?* That is how deep the memory had been repressed and how confused and severely disoriented I had become.

Her response to me was shocking as she became angry and told me to never say that in this house again. I immediately shoved everything down that was trying to come up and felt ashamed that I had even asked. (I suspect now it had touched her repressed memories of sexual abuse as well. And she was unable to handle it.)

I left the room knowing that there was no help for me. I had to keep it together because I was escaping soon and going to the university.

MY ROAD TO PERSONAL DISCOVERY BEGAN THE DAY I STEPPED FOOT ON CAMPUS

I was happy to get to the university, even though it was not the one I wanted to attend. I was still grateful that my father offered to fund my way through that university since it was his choice. I knew it was the last decision that he would make for me.

I felt a great sense of freedom that the university was hours away from home and I was finally on my own. I ran around barefooted and tried a little bit of everything, even drugs and alcohol for conventional use. I was experimenting with and exhibiting what I thought was personal freedom. Drugs never appealed to me, but there was the freedom that I could make my own choices. I even ended up living in a big hippie house with two psychotherapists who were married.

MY NEW INDEPENDENCE AT UNIVERSITY ALLOWED ME TO DISCOVER PARTS OF MYSELF THAT HAD BEEN KEPT HIDDEN FOR YEARS

While living in the big hippie house with the psychotherapists, I found myself putting posters of starving Ethiopian children on my walls instead of what all my colleagues had of rockstars and beauty queens. I found myself curiously drawn to remember that other people were suffering all around the world. I did not want to lose sight that I had it well in so many ways with food and water and a roof over my head. I knew I was blessed. I did not want to forget about other people and other places who were in less favorable circumstances and even, at times, great suffering. These posters helped me feel connected to others all over the world and to remember diversity. I wanted to do something to help other people.

The crazy professor with the curly wild hair would come up in my room and pull my starving posters down, saying that I was being a martyr. In my slight fairy way, I would rise and put them back on the wall standing up to his authoritarianism. I was done with people telling me who I was and what I could do or not. Something in me began to loosen up during this time, and it felt like a sparkle of who I was, some glamour of light and expansion. I was on my own and grateful to be out of the confines of what had felt like prison living with my family.

MY JOB AS A WILDERNESS PRESERVATIONIST SPECIALIST HELPED ME DISCOVER A DEEP CONNECTION WITH MYSELF, SPIRITUALITY, AND NATURE

In the summers between the University semesters, I worked for the National Forest and Park Services in California and Arizona and another native organization in Alaska helping Inuit children in a summer camp in the remote wilderness areas. I realized I had a great passion for native cultures and wildlands and wanted to study the psychology of indige-nous cultures. I was energized by other cultures' views of life, and of their unique cosmologies. I had a deep desire to travel the world and study other cultures, and how they thought, felt, moved, and viewed the world.

Even though I grew up in a fundamentalist Christian household I had always remained open-minded amidst the indoctrination.

I was impassioned by my work in the National Park and Forest Services, which took me to some of the most beautiful, wild places on the planet. I wanted to work my way up as a woman in the field to save wild lands. I deeply loved the wilderness in its profound stately solitude, magnificence, peace, and beauty.

Some kind of magic and spirit began to infuse me from those wild places. I wanted to do everything I could to preserve it.

I also loved the wilderness because I was left alone. I felt safe from the land of men, the South, and organized religion. These towering ominous mountains reignited my strength.

I pushed my body to incredible feats as I traversed thirteen-thousand-foot mountain passes in granite and snow in extremely rugged conditions. I worked long hours in the elements doing heavy labor. I was unknowingly trying to get something out of me. Hundreds of miles of roadless, wild, high country was my home. I felt most at home above the tree line in the alpine terrain, amidst towering snow-peaked granite mountains, and glistening lakes with the sun cascading through in silver slabs. It was there I felt the strength of my spirit. I felt a freedom within begin to expand and call my name, whispering me further from the homeland of my birth, Appalachia, to as far west of the Rockies as I could roam.

I went on the run. But little did I know at the time I was running from the demons of my past buried within myself. It looked like I was simply a gypsy nomad and curious young adventurer full of life and luster.

ITALY WOKE ME UP WITH ILLUMINATING DISCOVERY

Even though I loved spending time outdoors, I always longed to travel abroad. When my university sent flyers around campus for informational sessions about programs of study, I was the first to arrive. I longed to explore new worlds of opportunity.

Going away to Italy at age 18 by myself was another indirect attempt at healing. Deep down, all I wanted was to get as far away as possible from my family and the memories of abuse. I remember attending the first educational session describing the semester abroad in Italy. I applied and got what I thought at the time was my ticket to freedom. Even though I had no previous experience in Italian (my background was in French) they let me attend.

Leaving the Southern Bible Belt as a young unmarried woman alone was not easily accomplished, frowned upon, and outright discouraged. I had not yet recovered and was still extremely dissociated. The dangers were many, especially traveling alone. I was a young, blonde, naïve, female, and I did not speak the Italian language.

I anticipated the adventure of a lifetime and what they had described to us during the meeting. I flew away to the land of rolling green hills, ancient eloquent buildings, prolific cathedrals, beautiful people, and strong luscious wine. I had never before given Italy a thought. I suppose I would have gone to any far-off country if it was offered. I was young, on the run, and trying to escape my past, while I still could.

My angels must have been busy and had their work cut out for them. The anorexia was still in play and was exacerbated when I landed in Italy. I remained hidden in these anorexic/bulimic patterns for many more years including in Italy. I had met a handsome Italian man with dark wild curly hair who was charming and friendly. He reminded me of my friend, the college professor, whom I had lived with back in North Carolina. He befriended me quickly and started showing me this ancient city and sharing with me its history and culture. I fashioned myself a cultural anthropologist. By then I found it delightful to be able to speak some broken Italian with this intelligent man. I was intrigued by the new culture, the history, and the possibilities that I felt on this adventure. He led me into a building that he claimed had beautiful art regarding the Palio race and with my love of horses I was quite allured.

I thought it was a public space, but it was his private space. I was fixated on the unique architecture and structure of the buildings and the ancientness and the heaviness of the old door with the enormous wooden handles. Every structure seemed like a piece of art. I was mesmerized by the newness of it all. Everything had a bit of magic in it and was new and foreign. At this point, I longed to trust people. It was embedded in my nature, in my core. Throughout my young childhood, I was trained to become a people-pleaser. Yet, I started to feel something was wrong as I stepped through the door. Then he quickly locked the door behind me, and my skin began to crawl. I felt panicked deep in my core realizing he was another predator as he lurched towards me and began grabbing me.

I fought frantically, pushed him away, and was able to grasp the lock and open the door. I ran down the Medieval walled narrow corridor of Siena. This attack triggered my memories and pain. I started starving myself again. I was hardly able to ingest any food. My fellow students called my parents as they noticed me quickly dropping weight. I told no one about the attack. I was living a split life not realizing what was really happening at that time with the conscious amnesia. My friend simply told my father that I was not eating and dropping weight very quickly.

I felt betrayed by my friends at the time and just wanted to be left alone. When I heard my father planned to travel to Italy to visit me, my stomach dropped as if I was falling. It never occurred to me that I could ask him not to come.

My father flew over immediately to try to assist me. His solution was to take me on a mini vacation to resolve it. Clearly, he did not know what to do and thought if he could see me and make sure I ate, everything would be okay. I still find it odd that no one suggested looking at why I did not want to eat. My desire to escape had been sabotaged, at least temporarily.

MY MINI-VACATION IN ITALY WITH MY FATHER TURNED TO DESPAIR

I was declining rapidly when my father arrived and then what was supposed to be a beautiful trip to a beach outside of Rome turned into despair. While we walked down through the thick brush of the seaside further, and further away from the car, I had the strangest feeling in my stomach. I knew something was wrong. I felt we should return to the car. It felt like a gap between my mind and body, and I could not make a full connection to take action and return. It was almost like I was frozen or paralyzed and could not act on this premonition. So, I kept walking towards the ocean.

Upon returning to the car, we discovered everything inside had been stolen. I had all the belongings I had brought with me to Italy inside the car. What was most painful to me, however, was the loss of my journals. I had spent hours upon hours writing in my journals. They included my deepest, most inner thoughts. Inside those sacred spaces included my inner world, my photographs, and my musings.

This was the last trigger for me. I could not stand to think how thieves could steal our things. I created a vision of them sorting through our things and tossing away anything that did not have any monetary value to them. To me those things were priceless. These thoughts made me feel physically sick. It had deeply touched the past violations that I had not yet healed. This was another clue that something deeper was going on, as my response to this was extreme.

At this point, the abyss in me was being touched and beginning to pull me under it. The dam broke and the river of tears began. I could not stop crying. My father did not know what to do. I strangely felt sorry for him because I was so used to being the parent. I felt, even then, that I needed to take care of him. I felt, even in my moment of grief, that it was not right to show my distress or to be a child or be vulnerable or fall apart even once. I had never fallen apart in my family despite all that had happened to me. The level of stoicism was intense, and it felt like it was killing me. I was crying for so much more than that moment. The deluge had begun. I began to feel the untouchable loss of what had happened to me my entire life.

The U.S. Embassy took us in for the night. We had no money, no clothes, no food. We had only what we carried on our bodies. We spent the night in the Embassy in Rome. They were kind to us. They gave us provisions and the next morning, asked us to be on our way. By then we had also received wires of money from home. To everyone else, it appeared things were back on track. Yet, I had plunged into a dark, much-needed descent, clearly not about the things I had lost in Italy. My father had no idea what was happening to me and neither did I, really, at that time. He departed back to the States, with me in my usual form of stoicism saying "Everything is ok. I will be fine."

My father left. I retreated. I started walking around Italy like a numb shell, ghost-like, out of my body. This was the last trigger that my physical body could handle. My mind started to break open and leak out the repressed memories. I was unable to hold it in anymore. Everything was rising to the surface and bubbling over.

I HELD MYSELF BACK FROM THE EDGE OF THE SARDINIA CLIFF

Sardinia almost took me. What a beautiful, mystical island off the coast of Italy. It was a dramatically sculpted Mediterranean paradise that required a ferry crossing to get there. I am not quite sure what motivated me to go on vacation there alone. It was spring break from the Italian university. This was after our belongings had been stolen and my father returned to the United States. I knew I had hit rock bottom, and perhaps I needed to go on the run again. So, I roamed like a ghost over to this enchanted island.

When I arrived in Sardinia, I felt empty, alone, and searching but I did not consciously know what I was seeking. One day while in utter despair, I traveled to some of the most dramatic towering oceanic cliffs of Sardinia. Towards the edge I was overcome with the most overwhelming feeling of wanting to jump into the vast ocean below, to end it all, to free myself. As I stood on the edge of the abysmal cliff, eyes closed, everything seemed to stop and become quiet. I was only aware of feeling the wind, smelling the salty sea, and hearing the birds and crashing waves hundreds of feet below ripping into the craggy shore. I felt such pain, darkness, and lightness all at once as if my body was lifting up and away.

I began to take a step off the edge, in what felt to me like a dreamlike state. With full force, as I stepped forward, I felt a hand on my shoulder stop me holding me back with the message "*No, don't do that*". I turned around but no one was physically there. I felt the presence of something great with me, like a guardian angel, and its force holding me back from jumping. I knew at that moment I was being protected. It was not my time to die. Even though I had always felt death over my left shoulder as my adviser, this was not my time. Regardless of how many times it seemed I was begging for her relief and refuge; I was always protected. I had frightened myself, and this really shook me up.

I have had several of these near-death experiences during my lifetime. Each time I knew it was not my time to leave. I was always protected, stopped, or saved. I consider these moments in my life journey to be conducted by harbingers of grace, who have carried me during my darkest moments, and even today. They are partners on my journey to help me remember and fulfill my destiny and purpose here on Earth. I truly believe we all have them.

MY UNDIAGNOSED MEDICAL CONDITION STARTED A PERSONAL UNRAVELING THAT WOULD EVENTUALLY CHANGE MY LIFE

Pain is a formidable teacher.

There are so many kinds of pain, and everyone has a different version of the way they experience and relate to it. All I know is that it took me on a ride I will never forget and was one of my greatest teachers. Mine was physical pain, the nerve, in particular, that felt like a fire in my back, buttocks, and right leg. It was a call to attention; unavoidable, uncontrollable, and untouchable by supplements, medications, and nearly all medical and alternative healing modalities for a long time.

Beginning around age twenty it began. I was fit, strong, and robust. I still had the "Wonder Woman gene", so I pushed through. I came from a long, strong line of fiercely independent women, even though they were deeply traumatized. They did it all. They raised the children, worked full-time, and took care of everyone else on their own, at their own expense.

Working for the National Park Service in the deep wilderness I was accustomed to doing unfathomable things with my body. Twenty-mile days in rugged alpine terrain moving through snow, rock, ice, and drastic elevation gains were common. Sixty pounds on my back crossing alpine passes in all weather conditions was the norm. I reveled in my strength and ability to keep up with the boys as I was only one of two women in a large group of men.

There were few women employed in the National Park Service at that time, especially in the backcountry, and in some unconscious way, I was trying to prove myself equal to the men. I did not want to be seen as weaker or in any way less capable. In truth, as I look back now, I was not as physically strong as the men. I was clearly looking for approval and that I was *enough*. There was some deeper push of trying to prove myself, to my family, and especially my father, that I was "enough" because I had learned to be loved through performance. I had learned that "all love was conditional."

Out there I felt wild and free. My body was pushed to extraordinary limits. We were all pushed to our physical, emotional, and spiritual limits. I was accustomed to intensity, and in fact, probably addicted to it. It felt like the norm. This "temple of wildness" was preparing me and lending me strength for the healing work ahead.

It was not a single incident but a slow ache that turned into a deep burn. This deep burning pain in my sacrum, buttocks, and leg was becoming increasingly challenging. The crew boss recommended that I be sent out for medical care. I chose stoically to hike out the rugged 26 miles. Fortunately, it was down most of the way because I was stationed at 11,000 feet.

I realized I really did not know how to ask for or receive help. I did too much physically on that hike. It only made the pain worse. At the end of that trail was the nearest dirt road where I could get back to the forest station, and then get a ride into the nearest city of Fresno, California. There I continued to see a doctor, with the label of sacroiliac joint strain sprain, and proceeded on anti-inflammatories and physical therapy. This was all to no avail as my pain stayed the same and even began to worsen. I was then stationed on desk duty for the remainder of that season. It was getting worse and not better. I was profoundly aware that I was going into a depression. I felt I was losing my freedom because I had to be still and inside.

When this weak link cracked open in my back it left me with terrible, disabling low back/sacral and sciatic nerve pain. I was unable to lift a cup of tea when the pain flared up, nor could I sit for more than a couple of minutes. Most of my time was spent lying down.

When I was working at one of my park service stations, I met a professional mountain climber from Denmark. He was a fellow wilderness lover and we had fallen in love. In that kinship, we bonded deeply. We decided to go back to North Carolina where all my belongings were stored and continue my medical care. North Carolina did not have any medical answers for me, and my pain continued to worsen. The doctors had no explanation for why I was not improving.

After staying there only about six months, we decided to pack up the truck and drive across the country to see Olympic doctors in California. I could not sit for any length of time, so my partner prepared a space for me in the back of the truck, laying down pillows and pads to make the very long 3,000-mile journey.

We were going to try and find the medical answers to my mystery pain in California. We planned to do this on our way to Seattle, where he would pursue a wooden boat-building business, and I was going to try to heal myself. This happened in one great epiphany. I realized it was up to me and that I would have to "heal myself." I had no idea what that meant or how, but I knew I was on this path of self-healing.

I continued to see Olympic doctors in California, but again, to no avail. In California, I tried allopathic medicine as well as extensive alternative healing. Before arriving in California, I had tried every test possible for my condition including an MRI, CAT Scan, X-rays, Bone Scan, and Discogram. I sought medical care from medical experts all over the United States including multiple different manual exams from doctors. I had seen PTs, MDs, Chiropractors, Orthopedists, Bodyworkers, and Spinal specialists at top-ranked medical facilities with the best testing equipment, modalities, and innovative therapies offered at the time. I also did yoga, Pilates, lasers, and anything you could possibly imagine. I never turned down a recommendation from a physician or even a friend because my pain was debilitating and immobilizing. I even got my tailbone adjusted from within, which was unimaginably painful. I had been palpated and prodded with needles and hands and even tried many pharmaceuticals.

Nothing seemed to relieve the pain and most of these modalities made it worse. At the time I did not realize what I needed was not medical, but actual deep healing of the psyche. It was not a linear process but rather an unlayering process.

In their world, they could not explain why my back was not healing.

Little did I know that I had met my greatest teacher, my back.

Upon arriving in Seattle, I still attempted normal life. The pain was always there, relentlessly, firing down my leg. It was not the back pain that was so intolerable but the firing nerve pain radiating down my leg that kept me driving forward to find my answer.

It dawned on me that perhaps I needed to learn about my own musculoskeletal system, still thinking it was caused by something physical so that I could heal what was happening inside my body. I entered massage school in Seattle with this in mind. My hours were part-time, and I thought I could manage them. I figured I could stand or lie down during the classes. Everyone called me stoic during those years. All I knew was I had to find a way to discover what was causing this pain and a way to get relief.

A great surprise and alarming indicator came early on at massage school as I was receiving a session, and the practitioner went to work on my stomach. To my surprise, I began to cringe and freeze, and my skin began to crawl, feeling as if I would vomit. I asked the person to stop. This was a huge wake-up call and got my attention. I book-marked this moment in my mind as a signpost to something deeper that was living in me even though I was not quite ready nor capable of looking at it on my own.

When I discovered my love for the wilderness, I had also simultane-ously discovered dancing. Dancing allowed me to feel truly myself, whole and strong beyond measure. Dancing and being in the wilder-ness had begun to resurrect me. It was in those places that it was easiest for me to feel free, released, and uninhibited. Before the back pain, I would dance with abandon. I was still young enough to pursue a career in professional dancing. Unfortunately, this intense searing back/ nerve pain down my right leg that emerged during my work in the Park Service eventually prevented me from dancing for years. It became apparent very quickly after many years of seeking medical help and resolution for this condition that my body was in no state to pursue a professional dancing career. I was heartbroken at the loss of a dream between dance and the wilderness management profession.

I went deep into despair and depression from these losses. I became further aware of the chronic pain in my back and leg, along with the fact that I could not seem to find any resolutions. The losses seemed to start stacking up against me– one on top of the other. This was another unwanted turning point in my young life. Once again, my life's direction changed.

I was young but felt heavy and burdened with pain and trauma. My physical pain was unbearable, and nothing was helping. I wanted to have a childhood, to feel young and light, but it had been taken away from me. I kept telling myself those careers were not my destiny, or they would have come to pass. Even though I kept repeating this to myself, almost as a mantra, it did not reassure me at the time.

The pain in my sacroiliac joint and the resulting fiery sciatic nerve were directing my life toward my destiny. It caught my attention. At first, I resisted this pain. I was sassy, very willful, and stubborn. They say it takes something big to break hardheaded people and I guess I was one of those. I kept trying to get that pain to go away by any means possible and with allopathic medicine the pain only got louder, and I got weaker and more debilitated. I kept wanting to push it away and fix it. Back then I did not even think about listening to it or going towards it, or being curious about what it might be telling me. Eventually, I could no longer sit any length of time or even lift a light-weight object. I could barely get out of bed. My only semi-relief was lying down and even then, I still felt immense pain. Walking was confined to the shortest distance within my home. Pain had consumed my life.

FOR SEVERAL YEARS PAIN CONSUMED ME AND I WAS FORCED TO LIE ON MY BACK

At this point, I had been on my back for several years.

I felt like I might crack. I was stretched so far beyond my feeling of capacity that there was no "me" left. Darkness pervaded and I felt trapped there, yet I knew I had to stay awake, even in there, but I did not know if I could. It felt like bats were flying all around me, and my bones were creaking. In that unruly, dark place, I was isolated and untouchable beyond any words or any hands to be helped.

This is the surreal dreamscape that I had entered. It had become my reality. I was trapped in this shell of flesh and bones, pain searing. Nearly every moment I felt I could not take it. The hardest part was losing sight that it would ever end.

I was reminded of Frida Kahlo and her journey and how she had wanted to be cremated, not laid in a grave because she said she had laid down too much in this life from spinal injuries.

I too had laid down too much in this life. As much as I wanted to get up I could not, as the back and sciatic pain was too much for so many years. It would continue at later times in my life still to this day as I unload more memories and they process as pain in my back. Sometimes for months at a time, I would be laid out from the pain unable to do anything or even get out of bed. This continued off and on for 30 years. I dreaded the thought of having to lie down one more time.

The great awakening was that it was out of my control. What I came to realize was that everything was, to some extent, really out of our control. We can control our response and reaction to events. As we move through life, we are terrified to succumb to this idea of who controls what and relinquish truth to what I call, Source. My back taught me that.

The inability to move was a great teacher for me, in that I was such a mover and exercise addict. It was how I processed my emotions, cleared my head, and moved a tremendous amount of energy. It was how I was able to induce good feeling states in my brain with all the endorphins/happy hormones. It had become a crutch, a refuge, and a strong attachment. With all the body imagery issues that I had from the ritual sexual abuse; exercise had become a powerful coping mechanism. Without it, I would feel shame, unworthiness, and unlovability. I started to judge myself. I was not beautiful enough. I was not good enough. I was unlovable. When I could not exercise or dance, a part of me died.

In all those years lying down, the longing was so strong to dance, to run, and to be free. Physical pain has been one of my greatest teachers in this life. For a dancer and lover of "wildness" by nature, it took pain and immobility to get my attention.

All I knew was "I Am. Not this, not that, just I Am." This was a glimpse of my coming awakening.

MY BACK PAIN LED ME TO LETA ROSE WHO BECAME A GREAT MENTOR IN THIS LIFE

I began a deep descent into massive depression and suicidal ideation. I felt isolated and the chronic pain was unbearable. I thought endlessly about how to escape my body and how I could end my life. But something in me could not do it.

It was rare that I could get relief even through some form of anti-inflammatory or muscle relaxer and my body was reacting to pain medication. I discovered I was allergic to opioids and codeine and was having trouble finding other options that worked for my body. I wanted to die so badly and leave my body and escape the sensations that never seemed to end. But something kept me going. There was some light that was directing me like a hope that was whispering to me. It kept telling me to keep going forward and trust that I would find "the medicine" of what I needed.

Then one grace-filled day I met a man in Seattle in a bookstore who became a dear friend for many years. He said he knew a woman who was a channel and healer in the Seattle area. He knew he needed us to meet. By this time, I was 22 years old and had been in this pain for three years, immobilized. I felt I had lost, in a lot of ways, the youth of my life.

Channeling was not something I had heard of or experienced being that I was from a very conservative fundamentalist Christian background, which dogma never really agreed with me anyway. Yet, the heart of it did; the essence of love of God and prayer. Still, I was open to new things and to exploring and being curious. I was desperate. It felt right.

LETA ROSE HARNESSED A POWER UNLIKE I HAD EVER SEEN BEFORE

On a fateful day in the fall of Seattle, I entered the home of Leta Rose. As I entered the enormous silent house, I was ushered into an incredible room of brilliant color, art, and vibrancy. I sat down in the chair across from this powerful, unique, yet somehow familiar woman. Saying "woman" to describe this person is way too limiting, for what I experienced was her spiritual presence as a power. Yes, in many ways Leta was more otherworldly than human. I felt at home with her immediately. I felt a kinship, even though she also felt like one of the strangest beings I had ever met.

This beautiful towering six-foot Amazon-like build of a woman stood before me with a very unusual and otherworldly face. She explained to me that she would leave her body and a spirit guide named "Philo" would come into her body so that I could ask him questions and he would assist me. Somehow, I felt completely comfortable with this even though it was new to me.

I closed my eyes as she did. I centered myself in a deep meditative state, as best I could, even though I was in a great deal of pain. Suddenly, a powerful force came into her body and into the room itself. Her voice changed to a very deep masculine tone and foreign-sounding accent. Her eyes looked at me in a bold direct way different than before. It was undeniable to me that a great being had entered the space.

In a quiet, yet powerful presence behind closed beaming blue eyes a booming male voice emerged out of the woman in front of me. Words and energy cascaded forth.

Philo proceeded to ask me how he could assist me. I began with my questions. Of course, the most burning question I asked Philo was "What was sourcing this back pain"?

Philo looked at me through Leta Rose in the kindest, caring way and said to me "Beloved, you know what this is from, and it is time to remember. It is ok to remember now." I felt a surge of energy come down and through my body and I began to uncontrollably shake as deep undulating sobs emerged out of me, that had been held for so long. Tears streamed down my face as I let this energy take me shaking, releasing, and feeling for the first time.

As I collected myself after quite some time, I replied to Philo "The sexual abuse?" My voice was timid and shy, and terrified... and yet I had known this all along. Philo responded, "Yes, beloved yes, it is time."

I started to tremble. Instantly, my body shook, and my teeth chattered. Tears streamed down my face, and I began to rock. I was convulsing intensely, and it was like nothing I had ever experienced before.

This moment continued for what seemed like a lifetime but was probably only several minutes. I had been dissociated for twenty-two years of my life. (This happens in those who have had very severe young chronic abuse and trauma. The soul leaves the body, and the mind may create what is called "conscious amnesia" so that the person can forget temporarily, and this helps one survive the experience without dying or going crazy from shock and trauma.)

I was finally remembering that I had been ritually sexually abused repeatedly in the church. I was in shock and horrified. Memories were beginning to surface and flood my body. I finally knew what was causing the back pain, and that gave me some relief because there was an answer. It felt like I now could focus on this for healing. I was no longer wandering around in the dark searching for answers. This is why my lower back, buttocks, and leg had hurt for so long and were not recovering. There were memories, stored deep in the tissues of my body and there was a story in there that needed to be felt so that I could release it from my body and re-member myself. This is the story I am telling you now.

Philo shared with me many things, one of which was that I was a channel and healer myself. Even though this resonated deeply within me I still had a reaction of resistance and the feeling that I did not want such responsibility. It also felt like somehow this was the path that would bring healing to my back as well.

I was with Leta Rose and Philo for about an hour, but it seemed like an eternity. I did not want to leave that day. I wanted to stay with them because, for the first time, for as long as I could remember, I began to feel some relief. I felt like Leta Rose really understood me. I felt completely safe like I could be myself. I somehow understood completely every word that she said in the way that she spoke, and it felt like we spoke the same language. Something touched me deeply and I began to wake up.

What was inherently true in that first meeting is that we were deeply connected and made of similar ilk (fabric). It felt more like home than anything I could remember. There was a deep knowing and feeling inside of me that she was my kin or family. I had never experienced this type of connection.

Yet, my experience was challenging in many ways. The truth had been spoken and I was supposed to feel relieved. There had been a tension in my body and when it was uncovered, it felt like I was able to exhale for the first time in a very long time. But it was also the elephant in the room. This one took up residence in my back and lived there for a long time. The pressure began to release, even after our first meeting, but my journey toward self-healing was long and arduous. The body remembers even when the mind forgets.

Even though the perpetrators had used tactics to scramble my memories, my body remembered. My body and spirit were the doorway to remembering what had happened to me. The memories were stored deep in my cells and manifested as pain when it was time for the truth to reveal itself.

By our second meeting, it was clear to me that I was receiving my healing from Leta Rose and Philo was also training me.

I engaged in energy medicine, hands-on healing work, as well as channeling. After my first couple of meetings with them, I realized I had an innate gift inside of me that had been shut down and protected to keep me safe in my younger years.

These gifts would never have been allowed in my family; in fact, it would have been very dangerous to have shown that I had intuitive or psychic skills. I realized that I had an incredible ability to know certain things. I could feel and see energy. I had no idea I was as sensitive and tuned in as I was, even as a child. This explained a lot as I began to reflect on my journey. Leta Rose said she knew I had these abilities and that I was her apprentice. She knew I would be coming.

I BECAME AN APPRENTICE OF LETA ROSE TO BEGIN HEALING MYSELF AND BECOME A HEALER

Leta Rose and I decided that I would be her apprentice in all that she did: energy medicine, channeling, and shamanism. She kept telling me I was already a channel and a healer. I certainly did not feel that way. I did not feel like much of anything except a walking ball of pain. But something in me was waking up again and listening to this and remembering something ancient that lived inside of me. In pressing all the pain down, I had pressed these gifts down also. At first, I was resistant to this path. It felt like a huge responsibility and something that I did not want. I had different plans for my life. I still had hopes of becoming a professional dancer or perhaps to continue working to save wilderness lands. I was only twenty-two years old. I had dreams. Being a healer was not one of them.

My soul had a different idea. I was at another crossroads. Even after I began this work, my personality started kicking and screaming. After sitting with this resistance, and arguing with God for about a week, something in me melted. I realized I was being called to this path. I physically could not do the other careers or fulfill them because of the pain in my spine. I felt as if Source was grabbing me by my shoulders and pulling me by the back of my hair prompting me in a new direction. It was a visceral palpable feeling. I knew in my heart this was my calling.

I Finally Accepted My Purpose in Life Dedicating My Soul to Shamanism and Healing

My apprenticeship with Leta Rose was all-consuming and became my life. I had no guidance externally in the world until I met Leta Rose. I had not had a role model, mentor, or a positive influence up until that point.

I was far away from the South and in a new world of the West Coast. It shocked me how my life changed with my good fortune. Now I had support and guidance. I also had help to learn how to find my own inner knowing. Surprisingly a home came up for rent close to Leta Rose and I lived there for several years. For the next six years, I spent most of my time at Leta Rose's house.

MY FAMILY LIFE BECAME FURTHER STRAINED AS I BEGAN MY HEALING JOURNEY

Since I had spent several years *literally* on my back, I was unable to work. I was able to receive some disability supplemental income from the National Park Service. Still, there was not enough financial support to cover the increasing cost I was incurring. I was stressed about having enough money to be able to heal myself with all the care I needed. I did not have any place for financial backup. This was very lonely and frightening. Most of the months I could barely pay my rent, or have enough to eat, while still receiving medical care, doing the apprenticeship, and healing myself.

Sporadically through those early years, after the emergence of back pain, I would ask my father for financial support. But he made it very clear to me that he felt the symptoms were in my head and that I was making it up. He had some idea that I wanted handouts and he proceeded to offer me little amounts of support sporadically when I would ask. Soon, I began not to be able to tolerate receiving those little green bills of shame. It was the opposite of who I was, a hard worker and over-excelling in my younger years. Nothing had changed.

I had exhibited over-responsibility and perfectionistic traits that I was working hard to heal. But I realized my father could not see this in me, and I would never be able to meet his impossible criteria or expectations. I reminded myself that even back then before the disability, he was never satisfied with my accomplishments. I closed this financial door, to honor myself, and as I did that, my credit cards became insurmountable. I could not keep up with payments. Shortly after I declared bankruptcy.

Even so, I realized I was finally on the right path.

> We don't see things as they are, we see them as we are."
>
> — ANAIS NIN

> No problem can be solved from the same level of consciousness that created it."
>
> — ALBERT EINSTEIN

WITH LETA ROSE, I BEGAN MY HEALING JOURNEY

One of the greatest gifts Leta Rose gave me was to help me start re-entering into my body and to reconnect, cleanse, and bless all my (chakras) energy centers and meridians and circuits into a balanced state again.

She also helped me strengthen my auric field and weave the weak spots and holes back together again so I could have a sense of integrity and protection around my light body. When a person is abused or experiences trauma, the light body, also called the aura, fractures, and tears, leaving holes and vulnerabilities. I learned during these years deeply how to fill out my light body and strengthen it, so I was protected. In this way, it healed the psychic openness I had, which was out of balance, as I had been taking on other energies like a sponge, which often made me very sick.

Leta Rose also helped me work greatly with my level of discernment of who and what was safe to be around. I learned to pay attention to my internal meter of how I felt inside and act accordingly. She helped me see below the appearances of things into what was real and not real. She trained me diligently to focus on the actions, the energies, and the quality of people, places, and situations and not to get caught up in the words or how things appeared. She helped me learn to call upon my natural powers of invoking the unseen forces on behalf of myself and others for healing.

Leta Rose helped me refine my channeling ability. Mostly, I learned how to trust my own channeling and inherent ability. I learned discernment about who, and what I was willing to channel, and that I was in charge. In this way, I learned how to protect myself during channeling so extraneous energies are not brought forth. It is important to be incredibly discerning of the vibration and frequency of what you wish to bring forth.

I was taught extensively in the Toltec shamanic healing arts including the powerful technique of "Recapitulation" which I was required to do daily for many years. It is an energy/breath technique that retrieves the energy you have dissipated in any charged, or traumatic memory or by having done any habitual pattern. It clears any tendrils, hooks, or imprints from other persons or situations stuck in your light body. It also clears your energy body or light body of what the shamans call "heavy energy. "I did this for hours daily for years, clearing away the trauma and pain of my past. My homework was to recapitulate my entire life daily from the beginning until the present moment. This was a huge task. I still recapitulate to this day as needed. This allows you to move and act with more clarity, power, and freedom.

Recapitulation enhanced my power and navigation skills in the dream world as I was taught the art of dreaming and stalking and how to gather Chi, retain it, and cultivate more. Chi is another word for our essential energy that is stored most specifically in the Dan Tien or Hara and spread throughout the entire body overflowing into the energy body. The Dan Tien or Hara is the energy reservoir behind and around your navel where the core Chi is stored.

I was taught about the importance of how to use my sexual energy and that there was no such thing as a casual exchange of sexual energy. When you share sexual energy with another it goes into your light body, chakra system, and physical body. There is no such thing as casual sex even when people are not bonded or emotionally invested. You are still deeply affected by another's energy and must have awareness and skills in order to clear others' energy out and keep yours intact.

Most of all I was expected to be impeccable. Impeccability was my shamanic lineage and path. Impeccability is being clear and guided in alignment with one's actions and words at all times, never straying, and dedicating one's life to this cause. It is the right use of one's energy at all times. It is pure integrity and dedication to truth. One can never do harm.

Toltec shamans are impeccable. This was my Toltec lineage, and I was following this path of impeccability as best I could. I knew this was my truth, and that I had to stay the course. In fact, I did not even feel the ability to stray from it even if I had any desire. I was on a short tether and would be yanked back if the slightest distraction got me.

I was taught to work with the fifty-two layers of energy of the aura and to clear on eight levels including clearing and balancing chakras, performing etheric surgeries, clearing entities, residues, and interferences. This work included performing demonic and other entity depossessions. We worked extensively with medical issues, mental illness, abuse, etc. No issues were off-limits. All subjects are in the realm and affected by energy medicine.

To be a shaman was a great responsibility and the shamans often carried the burden for a whole group and community, as well as for the land. I wondered why anyone would want such a path. Often shamans would die young in native cultures. I was humbled by these teachings, and they reinforced the level of discernment, listening, protection, and impeccability that I needed to cultivate. This is an endlessly, ongoing learning that I practice daily.

CERTAIN MODALITIES CHANGED MY LIFE IMMEDIATELY

As a condition of my apprenticeship with Leta Rose, I was required to clear my own path. This was part of my healing and training. It was also important for me to learn and understand how these techniques worked first-hand so I could help and heal others.

Shortly after meeting Leta Rose, she introduced me to a world-renowned Naturopath, Walter Crinnion, who later would change my life and become my best friend as well. He also worked as a healer and did energy medicine work. Together the two of them began, through a series of sessions, to clear and release all the negative energies stored in my body from the ritual abuse. This was not a possession, as my consciousness was intact, but these dark energies from the abusers had been absorbed into my tissues. I received these healings for a period early on while I was apprenticing with Leta Rose until these influences were completely removed from my body.

Leta Rose helped me to remember who I truly am. In her presence for the first time, I felt like myself. I felt seen and that I was okay just as I was. I began to understand why I was having the experiences I was as well as the reason for my chronic pain and my different emotions. I began to understand my greater destiny and what I was here to do. It was such a gift to learn this at a young age and to feel focused on my life purpose already. I felt humbly grateful to be working with clients for many years who would come to me, at all ages, seeking their life purpose in life. I was grateful to have discovered my purpose so young.

ONE OF THE GREATEST GIFTS I LEARNED FROM LETA ROSE WAS "PARTS WORK"

Understanding, learning, and applying "parts work" changed my life.

One of the greatest gifts that Leta Rose gave me was to teach me "parts work." That's what she called it. It was a method of how to go inside myself through deep inquiry and meditation and listen and hear different aspects of my psyche at different ages. She helped me categorize each part by naming them and asking them who they were and their role. I did all of this by speaking with her, and as I became more adept, on my own, in my journal. Then we began to help each of these young aspects of myself to be heard and to get what they needed.

Through my inquiry into these different, and often very young parts of myself, I was able to give them empathy and information to begin to guide them. This was a painfully slow, challenging process that happened over years and years of work. I still engage in this process today and use it as needed to keep myself centered and to soothe any upset parts that might be triggered.

Parts work is a wonderful way to heal the fragmentation that I had incurred. Healing fragmentation: trying to bridge all the pieces of one's psyche back together was a whole other ordeal. That took many years of hard, devoted presence and work, which I am still doing.

At times different experiences would happen when accessing the child parts. I would shake, and experience temperature changes, vocaliza-tions, or flashbacks. At other times I would get temporarily stuck in a part of self, like a fragile child or protector part, and have trouble coming out. As working on my inner parts ensued, I worked with meeting all the parts within me. I learned their ages, names, and functions and helped them work together to be seen, nourished, and integrated.

I performed parts work extensively through writing in my adult years. This "inner parts" work was extensive and time-consuming. It took a lot of energy. I had chronic fatigue much of my life and this emotional work was very exhausting. I would spend much time feeling split and in conflict and had trouble making decisions. I had to accept long periods with no peace between the parts nor the ability to find peace in my core. The intensity of the memory recall and internal conflict of the fragmented parts was often too much to bear.

When I looked around, I realized that others did not deal with the same level of fragmentation. I would then begin to feel more discouraged and humiliated as I compared myself to other people. Humiliation was one of the deepest feelings that were chronic post-abuse. It became clear to me through research and experience that there was only a tiny percentage of the population that had this level of fragmentation and that it was isolating.

I discovered many years later that Richard Schwartz had created a beautiful system, called Internal Family Systems (IFS) to explain at length how this occurs and how to work with all the parts for integration. When multitudinous little selves are running around, yelling, pulling on the person in which they inhabit, and having opposing wants and needs, a sense of feeling fragmented is experienced. I expand more deeply on fragmentation in a later section.

I see fragmentation as a continuum where everyone falls into a certain place on the spectrum. Imagine two points with a line in between. The point on the left is the integrated whole Self and as one travels on the line to the right (which is the continuum) there becomes many more parts and fragments of self from trauma. Eventually, the furthest right point becomes multiple personality disorder which now is called dissociative identity disorder (DID). The younger your age when the trauma occurs and how often the trauma is repeated, coupled with the severity of the acts can determine the level of fragmentation.

Leta Rose recommended I read multiple books on shamanism, energy medicine, and psychotherapy. I had to do many shamanic practices daily. These practices consisted of different kinds of breath, movement, and energy techniques. I also had to journal daily about my inner process and any shifts I experienced. I also immediately began to participate in her client sessions learning how to do energy medicine.

I sat with her in these sessions and immediately started doing hands-on work as she guided me on what to do with the client while we worked together.

She would have me share with her what I was seeing in the client's energy field and physical body and what I suspected energetically was causing their symptomology. She guided me on how and where to move energy, and how to balance systems, organs, and levels of the light body.

I did not realize I had "seer" skills until Leta showed me what to do. She told me to look into people's light bodies and tell her what I saw, heard, and sensed. It was all right there, a whole world of energy, impressions, and even sounds. I had no idea I could do that until she had asked me to do it. She kept inviting me to do the next task of practice and to my shock, I could do it already. It lived within me as innate knowledge. It was natural to me. I felt like I was finally in my "zone," with the energy, channeling, and shamanic work.

When we channeled, she taught me how to open up and allow divine guidance to come through me for others. Shortly after, I began working with her clients multiple times a week. We decided I would receive bi-weekly energy medicine healings and channeling for myself. This was required so I could experience the work and understand it from the inside out. I also deeply needed this work. It was what I had been waiting for and it began immediately to help me.

My memories began to surface more quickly.

One distinct memory that was brought up for me happened in a horse stall where I was working.

I WAS GANG RAPED, YET IT WAS REFRAMED AS A HORSE INJURY AND NEVER INVESTIGATED

During one of my sessions, I discovered I never had a horse injury but had been gang raped by the cowboys in the stable where I boarded my Palomino Quarter Horse, Sierra.

The story of my injury had been reframed and told to me differently, of course. I had been told that I had pulled too hard on the reins and that my horse Sierra had reared up and fallen backward on top of me. I was told it was my fault. I was 17 years old, and my father had just bought me a horse. I frequented the ranch where Sierra, my horse, was boarded.

Three cowboys owned and ran the ranch. It was a father and his sons' tradition. I had been attacked by two of the sons in one of the stalls when I was mucking the hay out and cleaning the stall for my horse. One had come in, grabbed me, pushed me down to the ground, and began to rape me as the other intermittently held me down. He would then tend to the stall door to ensure there was no one coming. They took turns raping me while the other one guarded the door. I was coming in and out of consciousness. I was gasping for air and suffo-cating as the weight of their bodies smashed me down onto the scratchy hay igniting searing pain through my bruised body. I thought I was dead for some moments it seemed as I drifted out, finding myself rising up through a tall vast shaft of light way up into the heavens. Suddenly, I was in this vast place with light beings around me, and I thought I was dead. It is the most peace I have ever felt, and I looked at the light beings (spirit guides) and said, "I don't want to go back." The kindest most wise voice said, "Beloved, you are not complete, and you must go back." The next thing I remember is sliding quickly and furiously down a shaft of light slamming into my body gasping for my first breaths of air.

The cowboys stood over me telling me that my horse had fallen on me. My horse was nowhere in sight. Through my healing, I remembered and uncovered the mystery that these men had gang-raped me that day in the stable.

My parents were called that day and told that my horse had reared up while I was riding her, and she had fallen back on me. My parents then took me to the hospital where no one checked me for rape. My ribs were black and blue, and my inner groin muscle was torn. They told me that the saddle had bruised my stomach. My horse, which they said fell on me, had caused the groin tear from straddling her. There was blood and bruising all through my body which they attributed to the horse accident. I was sent home from the hospital on crutches.

All of these episodes occurred when I was still dissociated and had conscious amnesia. I was a *walking target.*

AS I WAS UNDERGOING MY OWN THERAPY, I FELT LIKE I WAS GOING CRAZY

Memory after memory kept pouring out of me during those sessions. I felt like I was going crazy, but the pieces of the puzzle were starting to also make sense. As the memories poured forth, they became more detailed and more prolific.

My body remembered. In the church cult, I remembered being drugged into sedation and at times blacking out, waking up very disoriented, not knowing where I was or what had happened. As I healed, I screamed. I cried. I vomited. I raged. My body shook uncontrollably, at times feeling frozen and immobilized, in a catatonic state, as I would retrace memory after memory.

At times I would even remember during the abuse having lost my voice and that I could not speak or cry out because I was frozen in terror. I thought I was going to die when the abuse was happening to me, and I really wanted to die. It felt like it lasted forever. I felt humiliated, exposed, and worst of all I felt like it was my fault. The abusers said that to me repeatedly. It was also a pattern that was present in my household where I was always being blamed and the scapegoat. I began to recover even more memories after the church experiences where I had been raped. I had become a walking target, out of my body, with that energy signature that says "victim" flashing like a neon sign over me. Once I met Leta Rose I was never attacked again. This being had truly saved my life.

This healing continued for many years where I received work from her and retrieved new memories that I had to feel, process, and release. It was the hardest work I had ever done and a true act of dedication. I knew I wanted to be free of the pain in my body that was keeping me disabled. Over time, after doing thousands of hours of this work, the pain in my back and leg began to decrease.

It felt like so much had been taken away from me, from my innocence, purity, trust, safety, and really my childhood. My body had been violated and overcome with toxicity. It could not process all of what had happened and was overwhelmed. I did many different modalities to heal including naturopathy, homeopathy, Chinese medicine, colonics, and more during those years including intensive therapy. I had been out of body for so long that once I started to remember and re-enter my body all these symptoms began to emerge. They were stored in the tissues of my body as repressed memories waiting for the time to be felt and processed, which was beginning now.

Since childhood sexual abuse was so prolific, extreme measures were undertaken to remove these foreign abuse energies from me. They had lived within me for so long. Dark entity beings had also entered my body hungry and devouring. At times they attached and located within my body and energy field for many years to come until I would come to know this, and thus have them extracted. I was not possessed by them as the abusers were, as they had not infiltrated my consciousness, since fortunately, that was intact. I was, though, deeply affected and interfered with by them which caused, as I have expressed throughout this book, much suffering, and challenges in my life. These dark beings impact one's thoughts and emotions, and create body symptoms.

Fortunately, these dark entity beings that parasitically stuck within me were not able to take over my core and were finally removed in my early 20s. This process of removal took time and was extensive. Vomiting, gagging, coughing, shaking, screaming, body pain, terror, and many other ways of releasing heavy emotions emerged from my war-torn vessel as these energies were extracted from my being and body with the help of Leta Rose and Walter. It might have looked dramatic from the outside, but it was simply the fact that these energies and feelings needed to be felt and released.

AN ADDITIONAL TECHNIQUE WAS PARTICULARLY USEFUL DURING MY HEALING PROCESS: EMOTIONAL FREEDOM TECHNIQUE/TAPPING

Emotional Freedom Technique, also known as EFT, was a modality that I discovered on this healing journey. It was instrumental in helping me work through deep overwhelming memories, body symptoms, phobias, and limiting patterns that were the result of abuse. I learned this new technique through a female mentor of mine who is a body-centered psychotherapist and ritual cult sexual abuse expert.

I was referred to her by Leta Rose 20 years ago and she began helping me understand and heal what had happened to me. At the time when I got her number as a referral, I began calling her and did not hear back. I called several times even after she told me that her practice was full, and I asked if she would be willing to ask Source if there was any possibility to see me. I felt a deep calling that she was my person to help me get further on my journey.

Finally, she checked in and got "yes" that she would take me on as a client, even though she had closed her practice to new clients. I felt blessed. She has changed my life. Grace intervened. She helped me navigate some of the deepest, most complex terrain of understanding and recovering that I have done regarding this type of family and cult abuse. I am in deep gratitude to and homage to her.

EFT is often fondly referred to as Tapping. In EFT acupressure points are activated by tapping along specific meridians (energy lines in the body) with core material statements while being expressed verbally out loud from a deep state of presence. This technique is very helpful for desensitizing and releasing the charge of anything heavy, painful, or where our wiring is mixed up. EFT is great for phobias, chronic conditions, depression, physical and emotional pain, insomnia, anxiety, weight issues, addictions, and many more things.

I integrate EFT into my practice today and I have found it to have helped vast numbers of people with innumerable conditions.

Through these mentors' guidance, support, love, and training, I learned how to access my intuition more deeply and to trust what I call "my knowing."

AFTER UNDERGOING THOUSANDS OF HOURS OF HEALING I UNCOVERED MULTIPLE REFLECTIONS

The importance of undergoing any kind of therapy for childhood sexual abuse cannot be understated. I was required to do it as part of my training to become a Shaman, but for anyone who has suffered any kind of trauma, it is the main path back to oneself.

THERE WERE SEVERAL OUTCOMES I EXPERIENCED FROM CHILDHOOD SEXUAL TRAUMA: I ATTRACTED THE WRONG MEN

Before I did the healing work, I unknowingly and continuously allowed myself to be vulnerable among people, especially men. Usually, these situations were dangerous, both emotionally and energetically, as well as fatiguing. Early on they were also physically dangerous. I endured a series of rapes after the ritual church abuse until my early twenties.

After meeting Leta Rose, I was no longer attracted to the physical danger of certain men but continued to clean up the internal mechanisms within myself that would have allowed past tolerance for energetic and emotional danger. I had to clear the energy signature, which was carrying this beacon, like a flashing light above my head. I learned to clear this very energy signature through energy medicine.

This has been a lifelong process of cleaning and clearing these early energy imprints to a very fine-tuned level in order to receive what is truly healthy, bonding, and connecting without being depleted, used, or harmed in any way. For a while, I went from too much tolerance to zero tolerance concerning any negative behavior from men. That is common for one to swing to the other end of the pendulum as they are seeking the balance of the middle path. Trauma creates extremes. **Healing represents a sort of middle path, where we have more bandwidth, flexibility, and ability to not be so extreme, and less reactive.**

My open energy field created many problems in my life because my boundaries were weak, and I was too trusting for many years. I was too open and tolerant.

Later as I healed my sexuality, I also had a propensity to be the healer in my intimate romantic relationships. It was like I had an inner dial set for helping men heal their sexuality.

I had to be careful because I was so accustomed to nearly always experiencing a problem with sexuality. I was attracting that for a while because I was "normalized" to it.

It might seem paradoxical, but the abuse had the opposite effect on me in some ways. It was like something in me knew whole healed sexuality innately and nothing could tamper with that nor take it away from me. It was like I had a meter inside that could tell when something was slightly off in the programming of someone's sexuality, including my own.

My main "job" regarding it was to work on cleaning up my energetic boundaries. I had to become aware of no longer letting people feed off my energy. I was conditioned in the abuse and in my family by people continually feeding off my energy. These abusers were not sovereign unto themselves and continually drew strength from me even as a child. They lacked energy and they needed someone else's energy to survive.

HOW I WAS ABLE TO HEAL MY SEXUALITY

After meeting Leta Rose and starting my healing journey, I soon discovered that I could hardly receive physical touch from anyone. It would trigger memories. It took some time to be able to receive touch anywhere on my body from a woman or man. This was one of the worst results of the trauma. As I mentioned earlier, I first experienced this when I was in massage school being massaged by a female practitioner.

I was determined to reclaim my own natural sensuality and pleasure, which was mine, and not allow my past to have stolen that from me. I went on a mission to heal my sexuality. I was determined to resolve this for myself. I began a process of slowly re-patterning and desensitizing my body to the touch trigger by receiving an appropriate healing touch and creating conscious rituals for sexual healing.

Dr. Walter Joseph Crinnion became instrumental to me on this journey. At our first meeting, he asked me: "What happened to you in your past?" "You are so young and there are a lot of medical issues that you already have." He sensed something deeper had happened.

I proceeded to tell him my story. After hearing my story Walter stopped in his tracks, tears streaming and welling up in his eyes. He said "Isa it's coming to me to offer you a healing. I have a men's group and I would like to see if they would be willing to hold space for you so that you can share your story and have the protection of the sacred masculine." Tears streamed down my face as I quietly began to weep. He then reached into his pocket and pulled out the rose quartz heart rock that he had carried most of his life. It was given to him as an amulet for feeling safe. He said from that point forward I could carry this rock as a reminder that I was eternally safe and that he would be with me. I could not believe this doctor who barely knew me, was offering such care and kindness to me. It was in Seattle upon meeting Leta Rose and Walter that the floodgates had opened in support. I was in shock by all the blessings and helpful energy coming towards me.

I then received direct guidance from Source to create a shamanic ritual to release the sexual abuse memories from my physical body while Walter's sacred group of men would hold vigil and protection around me. As mentioned earlier in this book, I was abused ritually in groups of men as a child, so I decided to heal myself with this powerful ritual in a group of safe, honoring men. May these men be blessed forevermore.

I RECEIVED HEALING FROM THE PROTECTION OF THE SACRED MASCULINE

As the men surrounded me, with their strong, bold hearts, beaming newfound safe presence at me, I felt deep shaking in my body, extreme vulnerability and terror arise. Still, though, I knew this was an opportunity. I was barely able to speak, and my voice cracked. But I proceeded to tell my story of what had occurred in the past ritual sexual cult abuse. These men met me with a kind and powerful loving demeanor. They held such compassion and a fierce protection for me that I had never before felt. They apologized for all men and expressed their empathy for me. They let me know they were here for me and holding a new space. I was already changed forever. Then I rose to enter the enclosed healing room as the deep full sound of drumming droned from the previous space. I heard the eight men call in the spirit of protection and healing for me.

I was placed on a massage table in the next room with rose petals surrounding and under my body. In this healing room, I had two women supporters, Leta Rose, and another, as I lay naked a man I had chosen entered the room to sacredly anoint my body with specific healing oils. He first spread rose petals all over me on the healing table. The intention was to bless and anoint my body everywhere including all the places where I had been abused. These sacred oils were blessed with all our prayers and through intention was to release any leftover, stored abuse energy in my tissues and to re-sanctify my body as a holy place.

I was a shivering rush of emotions, as memories flooded my body. My only job was to breathe, which was difficult at moments, and feel my emotions as well as stay in my body as it shook and trembled and discharged.

The men drumming and singing in the other room carried me and cocooned me in a safe bubble of healing light. The women caressed my body rubbing my brow and brushing the tears and sweat away while soothingly, holding my hands and gazing deeply into my eyes offering nourishing and comforting words. I was told I was safe, supported, and held in love and that all the terrible things that had occurred were leaving my body now. I was reminded that the abuse was finished and now was the beginning of a new chapter of my life of all goodness and well-being and safety and connection. I sobbed and sobbed, weeping, for all the years of being alone and terrified.

I had been ritually abused in groups and now I was being healed in a Shamanic Ceremonial group. I was changed that night. I left blessed as a sanctified woman and was never the same again. I was coming home to my own body as a sanctuary now, not a war zone. I could start to reclaim my sexual pleasure. It was mine.

This began a long chapter in my life of consciously healing my sexuality. From this time forward I did sexual re-patterning exercises regularly with my romantic partner. These exercises were given to me by Leta Rose and my therapist.

It took many years for me to be able to have a comfortable, deep, and intimate sexual relationship. It was very slow for quite some time. The repulsion of sex was overwhelming, and even a level of grotesqueness would arise. I would freeze and could not speak and would go numb and collapse into a heap on the bed. The shame I felt of humiliation, and exposure was immense. I thought at times that I would never get there, and I almost gave up.

Thank God for the good men over the years who were patient, held my hand, and reminded me that I was beautiful. I hated my body so much because of what it had been through and what had been put into it. I could not separate the two for quite some time, my body, from what had been done to it.

Through the good men in my life, I learned to love my body again and see it as beautiful and a place of deep pleasure, connection, and an ecstatic realm of union with God. By some holy miracle, many years later, after much focus and commitment, I had full deep intimate sexuality back. I was in awe of what is possible.

I recall a conversation with a dear friend of mine who is a Naturopathic Doctor specializing in women's health. She said to me, "Isa, you have the most healed sexuality of anyone I've ever met." She had known me for some years and had followed my progression down the healing path. The tears started streaming down my face and didn't stop. I thought, if you only knew what I went through to find that place in myself. And now I knew I had that gift to share with others.

Finally, now, after all this work, I felt I had gained the courage to fly home and disclose to my parents the long-held secret.

> Great lions can find peace in a cage. But we should only do that as a last resort. So those bars I see that restrain your wings, I guess you won't mind if I pry them open."
>
> — RUMI

AS I GATHERED STRENGTH DURING HEALING I WANTED TO REVISIT PARTS OF MY WOUNDED PAST: I RECEIVED THE RESPONSE FROM MY PARENTS I EXPECTED

My parents did not protect me, much less save me back then or later. I do not blame them for this, as I know they did the best to their ability given their upbringing and their trauma. They did not know this was occurring in my life even though they were delivering me to evil, the perpetrators.

At age 26 I flew from Seattle to North Carolina on one mission, to finally disclose to those who were supposed to have protected me (my parents) the long-held secret of the ritual sexual abuse that had occurred all those years ago, during my childhood. My mission was straightforward but not simple, "speak the truth "with compassion and courage, and as I did, I feared their world would shatter. I was terrified of what would happen to them and their response. I had been protecting them all those years at my own expense.

I worried about their fragility, of them blaming me, of not believing me, and of them abandoning me again. I was prepared that I might receive such an outcome. Unfortunately, this is what occurred. They even said it could not have happened. My father said that therapists had planted it in my head and that he could not live with the thought that he did not protect me. And I replied, "Yes, Dad, that is true you did not protect me, and I know how hard that might be for you to hear." Still, he dismissed that it had occurred and held that I had made it up and he was not willing to talk about it. Then to my astonishment, my mother changed the subject to the weather. No one wanted to talk about it, and it has been that way ever since.

That was the end of the story for my parents at that time. They did not ask me how I was or how that might have been for me or even if I needed anything. It was simply a five-minute conversation. In fact, they made it very clear they did not want to discuss it again.

One might ask, why did I wait so long to come out to my parents? I waited four years after beginning to have memories and realize what had happened to me in my youth before I spoke out to my parents. I waited because I was terrified, and I needed strength and understanding, and to do this at the right time for myself. I also had to deprogram myself through therapy and healing of all the memories of the abusers telling me they would kill my family or harm them in some way.

Also, in my family, it was not supported to speak about how you felt or about anything intimate or vulnerable or to have feelings. Even that one time I had approached my mother, questioning if I had been sexually abused, I was shut down. I risked that I would re-traumatize myself, reaching for help from people who had never been there for me before. This is what occurred. Fortunately, I had prepared myself for this and the letdown was a little bit easier.

I finally realized I was an orphan.

MY VISIT TO THE CHURCH THROUGH A TWENTY-SIX-YEAR-OLD LENS

As I was traveling through Italy during my freshman year, ironically, I was most drawn to churches, cathedrals, and holy shrines even though my church was the biggest nemesis of evil I had experienced. I would go within them to sit, pray, and reflect for hours amongst the pillars and spires of God. The only church that I despised was the one that had imprisoned me in abuse for all those years. It took me eight years from the time of leaving North Carolina to re-enter that church again.

Returning to the North Carolina church alone, I walked every corner, hall, room, Sunday school building, and parish hall and faced the demons of the old memories of that horrid place. My knees shook, my skin crawled, memories clawed and screamed from within to get out, and I froze and trembled as I walked through from one hallway to the next.

Looking through my twenty-six-year-old eyes I would tell myself: "It is over now. Those evil people are gone who did all those terrible things to me. I made it. See, it is okay to look now". My body shook. I felt cold and sweaty as fear dripped away melting like icicles.

This was mine to do alone. If I learned anything from this it is that you do not need anyone else's acknowledgment, response, or input to heal. You alone are enough. No matter what others project, believe, or judge, you can know your truth. Your body remembers and knows what to do. You can heal.

My body remembered, by collapsing and expressing symptoms to reveal the truth. My mind was the last to put the pieces together. It was like a messy mixed-up puzzle of fitting pieces here and there, but totally nonlinear and out of order, chaos.

For others, it may happen differently. Some people may be repressed or dissociated throughout life and when this happens eventually the emotions must be felt, or the person may start exhibiting disease.

I would often wonder back then why I could not remember the normal/positive things that people would recall about their child-hood. I mean I knew there were good memories too. People would ask me normal questions about my past, and yet it would be blank for me. **The neural pathways of negative memories have intensity and create thicker and deeper grooves than positive memories.** I have found that it overrides the positive memory recall until you can process enough of the negative memories in order to allow the positive to resurface. Thus, trauma memories have a way of taking over until they are healed. It is normal for people with this kind of abuse to not be able to remember much at all in their past, even good memories, and to walk around feeling triggered by nearly everything. That is why so many people choose to be alone or limit their contact with other people, to limit this possibility of triggering. A system can only take so much, and when it reaches beyond your bandwidth, then it can be hard to cope.

To this day there are still some missing pieces and holes within my memory. The nature of memory is erratic, elastic, and changeable. When they are ready to emerge, memories will spontaneously emerge out of sequence, as they are triggered by many factors.

This can be problematic. It leads to many victims doubting their own experiences because of the way trauma alters their brain chemistry and creates mental distortion. You can trust yourself as your body speaks to you and reveals messages.

AS I CONTINUED MY HEALING JOURNEY, I EXPERIENCED SEVERAL OTHER EMOTIONAL TRAUMAS THAT I HAD TO CONFRONT AND FACE: I EXPERIENCED SELF-HATRED AND SHAME

One of the terrible consequences that can result from severe childhood abuse is turning in on oneself in self-hatred and shame. This can be amplified by the fact that many victims of sexual abuse may also have orgasms during abuse. You read that right. That is what I said. This is quite an off-limits topic that no one wants to speak about. But it happened to me during heinous acts of rape. The body does what the body does, when stimulated it responds just as bodies do. This is not in your control. There is no shame in this, and it is not your fault.

Most people have shame to some degree, at least unconsciously and those who experienced severe circumstances early in life tend to be plagued by it. The resulting anger from having been so harmed is a form of intense energy that has to go somewhere, and for disenfranchised children, it is not safe for that anger to be directed outward. So this anger or excess energy gets directed inward against the self, playing itself out in a myriad of ways.

Often it results in a form of body dysmorphia. Body dysmorphia is when one cannot see their body clearly as it is. There is chronic fixation of it not looking okay or good enough. This can be a severe distortion. For example, a very thin person may look in the mirror and see only fat and feel they are disgusting. This hatred of the body includes shame, the feeling of looking awful or feeling disgusting, broken, messed up, or feeling some deep internal wrongness or defect. I experienced this severely.

What is needed is the releasing of this energy or anger outwardly, not inwardly towards the self or body. First, it is important to understand and name it out loud. "The feeling of self-hatred is coming from the past abuse." Then one can allow the energy to flow outward by breathing and letting the body shake, growl, yell, hit pillows, etc. and by using the breath in a conscious rhythm you can effectively release and transmute the energy. Inhale the same amount as the exhale in a continuous way.

For me, it arose as a feeling of profound ugliness, grossness, and the illusion of being fat. The anger would turn towards myself and the impulse to hit me, especially on my lower body, specifically my thighs and buttocks would arise. This was the area where so much of the abuse memory was stored in the acts of torture and rape. The desire to self-mutilate my body was very strong. I used to fantasize about cutting. Instead, I would hit myself with my fists several times on my thighs but then it would shock me out of the trance, and I would stop.

I would often have a fear that some disowned part of my psyche would take me over, grab a knife, and begin cutting me. At these times it was hard to look at sharp objects and I would avoid having any near my bedroom at night.

I had been known to have somnambulistic tendencies and would often be up and walking in my home half asleep, in an in-between state in the middle of the night. I used to fear that I would wake up in this state in the night and not be able to fully awaken and begin harming myself in some way by overdosing on pills or mutilating my body in some form.

Of course, these were horrible fears internalized from the traumas of what had happened already, I did not end up doing these things. For some survivors, consciousness fractures and the self-hatred does lead to self-mutilation and cutting. The cutting becomes an outlet to help one cope with the deeper overwhelm which is intolerable.

These fears were the memories internalized of what had already happened through the abusers. They were also sourced from everything that seemed out of control, which had been internalized. Still, for some time I could not sleep with any sharp objects visible. I had trouble sleeping in general.

For quite a long time I had night terrors. I would awaken abruptly from a deep sleep screaming and panicking as if something awful was happening to me in the moment. I knew this was my nervous system trying to release the memories of what had occurred. At these times I would awaken and have numbness through my extremities. Often whole limbs would be numb, an arm and a leg and I would have the feeling that I was immobilized and trapped. This simulated the feeling of abuse and feeling I could not move and would create a panic for me.

Sill halfway asleep, I would jump out of bed frantically, scream like a dying animal, and try to move my body parts. But I could not because my whole leg and arm would be numb. I would fall to the ground when my leg was asleep. Usually, in minutes my body parts would regain feeling. I would begin to calm down and wake up realizing where I was and that I was truly okay.

This happened weekly for several years.

It is common for survivors of abuse to not be able to sleep at night. Sleep is a form of letting go, and in abusive circumstances, sleep feels out of control. There may be a feeling of needing to stay awake to therefore be in control and aware of what might happen. This hyper-vigilance may extend into every part of one's life.

The longing for things to be stable, known, and thus predictable is very strong for survivors. The feelings of "out-of-control" from the past abuse manifested in most areas of my life. I became plagued by the internal feeling that everything was always out of control inside of me. It felt like through massive symptoms being exhibited in my body "it" was trying to take me over and kill me. I had absorbed the chaotic uncontrollable energy and was acclimated to it. I was familiarized with intensity and danger.

For a child, it is very hard and almost impossible to separate what is happening in the outer world from who you are in their inner world. The two become merged and you may naturally believe that every-thing happening to you is your fault. Children are naturally egocentric in their strengthening and building of a self.

Children need to control things, to know what to expect, and the learned perfectionism set in early. If I could make things happen or be perfect, then perhaps the bad things and events would not come. If I could simply anticipate the appropriate action and response, then perhaps danger could be averted. Yet, of course, that did not change it.

I felt a chronic sense of over-responsibility as if it were up to me to fix everything. There was simply no one else available to help me, protect me, or care for me. My parents were checked out. There was no modeling of a healthy way of being, nor explanation for what was happening. Everyone in the outer world was acting as if everything was okay.

I was told that everything was my fault. Therefore, whenever I encountered anything new and it went awry, the natural assumption was it was my fault. There was nowhere else for the energy to go except inward, against the self.

I EXPERIENCED SELF-OBJECTIFICATION

As a result of the abuse, I was hyper-focused on my body. The images were distorted. I was trying to see how I could get my body to look a certain way, feel a certain way, and even measure up as compared to others or some social norm. "You won't love me if I am not a certain way."

Massive billboards are everywhere of the perfect woman and man, body type and class, or even label, according to some subjective collective standard. Magazines, movies, music, and information everywhere — we are assaulted with the message:

"This is what is important and should be your focus."

"Have this and you will be happy!"

The challenge is that most of this influence lives deep within each of our psyches passed down through our lineage and comes to us through subliminal messaging daily.

What I learned was to ask myself a series of questions:

What does it take for me to be whole?

When do I experience moments of happiness?

What helps me be joyful and purposeful?

What brings me peace and sustained happiness?

I also learned that my state of being was the most important factor in my happiness. Then I could meet anything with equanimity, and I was no longer trapped by needing the moment to be a certain way, which was out of my control.

" Everything has its wonders, even darkness and silence, and I learn, whatever state I may be in, therein to be content."

— HELEN KELLER

AGORAPHOBIA WAS ONE OF THE HARDEST EFFECTS OF TRAUMA FOR ME TO HEAL

Later as the memories resurfaced, I experienced agoraphobia (an extreme and irrational fear of leaving your home or entering places that are hard to escape from or being in large crowds) for several years in my adult life. I could not drive beyond a small radius from my home within 5 to 10 minutes or so and the highway was out of the question. The sense of entrapment on the highway where exits were far away and the feeling of not being able to turn around was so overwhelming that I could not breathe. I would perspire into a soaking wet sweat with my pulse exploding and pounding in my chest as my lungs constricted my breathing. Planes, public bathrooms, and elevators were out of the question for several years as well.

I wanted to be free more than I was afraid. I had to say to myself "Even if moving through this and facing it kills me, then so be it, because I cannot keep living like this." I would have rather died than live any longer in that state of restriction where I could not go anywhere.

For several years I worked intently to heal agoraphobia. I avoided all pharmaceuticals even though silently I deeply wished there was a drug that would free that terror from within me. My body did not fare well with most pharmaceuticals and the side effects and often allergic reactions prevented me from utilizing them. Even alternative products, herbs, and homeopathic remedies really did not touch the panic. I clearly had to feel all these memories and repattern them that caused the agoraphobia.

Several years into doing this work with my counselor and preparing myself, I hired her to fly on 4 airplanes with me in a three-day period so I could face this terror (of being trapped in a small space - claustrophobia) the airplane triggered. We utilized the emotional freedom technique (EFT) and body sensory exercises to get me through that journey. Still, I felt the sweat pouring down me with my heart pounding. I almost ran off the plane hyperventilating, crying, and shaking while she held my hand. I felt as if I would truly die. Four planes later the terror lessened and several months later I took a five-hour flight to Hawaii alone.

Slowly from that point on bathrooms, driving, elevators, etc. became easier and easier. Traveling on airplanes had perfectly mimicked my sense of entrapment, being alone, and with no way to get help. When I was experiencing that I felt I could have died. These qualities all mimicked the exact feeling I had experienced during my past abuse. Memories often find a way to be processed.

> Terrified every moment of my life – and I've never let it keep me from doing a single thing I wanted to do."
>
> — FRIDA KAHLO

AS I PROCESSED MY GRIEF AND LOSS AND STARTED SHARING MY STORY WITH OTHERS, PEOPLE BEGAN TO ASK A LOT OF QUESTIONS

Why didn't I turn in the perpetrators?

People would later ask me why I did not turn the perpetrators in and go after them? I considered it. In fact, I often still consider my options, if I am being honest. I still suffer moments of trauma when I recall the events that occurred and how I can best show up in the world as both a healer as well as an advocate. I have evaluated and meditated on this for quite some time. Now, as a shaman and a healer, I rely on my training and experiences with others as well. I rely on my connection with Source for guidance, and from my therapist, as well as my own self-reflection.

So many years after, I know that there is likely no evidence I can point to of the abuse occurring, and more than that, few witnesses if any would be willing to step forward. I also know from many other cases that victims who report past childhood sexual abuse are often dragged through immense pain, threat, shame, and doubt. Their life is often made difficult by bringing this into the courts, where it causes them great pain on top of what they have already endured. I did not want to go through more pain, knowing that there was another path I could take, here, by sharing my story.

I also did not want to bring suffering to my family and those who would be impacted by this investigation. After all, I did not receive much of a reception from my parents when I visited them several decades ago and our relationship has not grown since that time.

I also knew that the preacher of the church where I was abused, had been fired from our church and left the area. By the time I woke up to these memories, it was over a decade later. I was guided by Source, and it was clear to me to do my own healing. I was guided to speak out through my story as it could benefit many people – not only the victims of abuse, but others who may be a part of their lives, who can see more quickly the signs and be able to lend support to those who are being abused or had been abused.

How did my family not know I was being ritually abused for so long?

As I reflected on my abuse, I realized that my family setting provided the kind of atmosphere for the abuse to take place.

Once I uncovered the ritual cult sexual abuse, I wondered how the perpetrators had gotten to me, since my mother and father were not part of the cult. This was the church that our family belonged to in the deep southern countryside, the middle of nowhere, on a hill far away from any town. On the outside everything looked normal.

But, in my family, no one listened or paid attention. In such denial, my parents chose appearances or optics – the desire to look good and always acted as if everything was okay. This was the exact breeding ground that made me vulnerable to being prey for perpetrators. My parents unknowingly delivered me regularly in my youth to the predators at my church in the deep South. They thought they were delivering me to God but were delivering me to evil.

Upon continued reflection, I realized that my parents' dysfunctional response to their trauma allowed secretive perpetration to occur which is exactly how family/lineage trauma is passed down. To top it off, it was all "in the name of God" by the perpetrators. My conservative Lutheran family continued looking good, pleasing others, and stayed silent. That was the family code. Of course, their bodies with some animation were moving about, making sure my physical needs to some degree were met, at least food and shelter, as well as taking me to school and church.

My parents had both disappeared unto themselves. Mother was "dissociated/not present" herself and told me much later that her father had sexually abused her and that he had at one time put a gun to her head and threatened to kill her. She claimed she had forgiven him. But I could not feel forgiveness in her growing up as a child or a soft place to lay my head. All I felt was cold brittleness and terror.

How does this kind of ritual childhood sexual abuse go unrecognized?

If something is out of your awareness of possibility then you are not looking for it, nor necessarily able to see the signs of it since these offenders are often so skilled and secretive in what they are doing. Many times, these rituals and acts have been passed down through generations polishing their expertise. It is only in more recent history that ritual sexual abuse has even become acknowledged as occurring, even though it has been a documented occurrence in many cultures across the world for generations.

Often a victim's hardest stage is:

"Did this really happen to me?"

"I must be making this up, maybe I am crazy."

When a victim wakes up to the memories it is like shaking off a fog and letting the dust settle. You begin to clear the way so you can get all the debris off, and out of you, and then you can see and move more clearly, not being influenced by the old internal programs. Many people will have a lot of opinions about what you are doing, and some may try to stop you. I encountered a lot of the following questions and scenarios:

- That did not really happen.
- This could not have possibly happened because I don't understand it.
- That is too crazy.
- You just want attention.
- A therapist put that into your head.
- You must get over that.
- It is the past. Be done with it. Just ignore it and don't feel or think about it. Then it will go away.

You cannot move on when this "something" has infiltrated the cells in your body, mind, and emotions. Your body does not lie. If it had not been for my body getting my attention, I would have probably ignored it all. Even if you do not think about it or feel it you can bet it is running your life unconsciously.

If you have not been a victim of severe trauma, it is best to not assume you know what is true for another person. Do not go immediately to doubting, even if it seems that you cannot understand how such a thing happened and even if the person's memories are not coherent or even make sense to you. You can help the most by being patient, holding space for them, and allowing them to reveal memories at their own pace. It may seem unspeakable to them and terrifying. Be a safe place with an open heart and help them to trust themselves. Of course, suggest resources to them and even perhaps groups or therapy. Getting help in the situation is imperative.

THROUGH MY MANY YEARS OF THERAPY, ATTENDING WORKSHOPS, AND NOW AS AN ADVOCATE, I REALIZED THAT BACK THEN I HAD BECOME A WALKING TARGET

It is classic that perpetrators seek people who exhibit weak, vulnerable, victim-like qualities. It is akin to animals hunting in nature by picking out the weak, old, sick ones. I certainly had "victim" written all over me. I was out of my body and not home. Another susceptible quality that I had was innocence and naivete.

The paradox is that I continued to display my essential nature of sweetness, softness, and vulnerability despite the heinous crimes. My internal protectors of discernment left me unguarded. They had been broken down and disarmed.

I also played the role of caretaker well. I was the strong one in my family, the caretaker in so many ways, and more adult emotionally than my parents. I had a double life and it split me, into more than two pieces. My duality has taken a lifetime of dedication to reintegrate. And still, I am reintegrating.

TWO INNATE COPING MECHANISMS OCCUR DURING TRAUMA THAT KEEP A VICTIM "SAFER" YET A VICTIM: THE IMPORTANCE OF KNOWING ABOUT STOCKHOLM SYNDROME AND TRAUMA BONDING

The nature of crimes like these is that they go unspoken and hidden. Cults are clandestine by nature. Many times, cult members have spent years and sometimes generations cultivating the act of secrecy. Abusers intentionally scramble the memories and cognition of the victims through brainwashing, programming, torture, drugs, and threats of killing. All of these tactics create distorted memories, overwhelming body sensations, cognitive dissonance (when someone is saying one thing but doing the opposite), extreme separation, and confusion within children whose bodies and brains are still forming. Receptivity and formation are at their highest in childhood. Cult coercion, "obey or suffer" or in some cases "obey or die" is followed by the victim often without resistance due to fear of retribution.

In these kinds of abuse, a child's life depends on the perpetrator, and this is what seals the bonding and even the child or adult victim may begin to care for the perpetrator, for their concern and pain. Because death is in the perpetrator's hands, the young child or adult innately begins to bond with the perpetrators in order to survive. In fact, the more violent the act the more bonding that occurs. This is referred to as Stockholm Syndrome and it affected me for many years. Unfortunately, a victim begins to protect the perpetrator because their life depends on it.

Stockholm Syndrome is to ensure the livelihood of the victim and their survival. At that moment the victim's survival is solely in the hands of the perpetrators. This is how such a violent act simultaneously is deeply intimate and primal even though completely inappropriate with any human, especially a child. Without the fully formed ego in a child, this creates deep cognitive dissonance and confusion about connection, love, sex, and boundaries. In children, the survival instinct is to feel safe somehow and this is the psyche's way to create that as best it can.

HOW TRAUMA BONDING PLAYS A ROLE FOR A VICTIM IN SURVIVING

In my desperate pursuit to survive, after trying to fight back and resist, one unconscious survival mechanism that began to happen in the beginning was to "trauma bond" with my perpetrators. This was not a conscious mechanism, but an unconscious automatic survival mechanism that simply happened out of necessity in order to survive. I didn't even know I was doing it until years later well into therapy.

Also, confusion about love occurs in this bond as well, especially when sexual abuse is present. As a child, I thought innocently that my love might be able to heal these crazy men and that this might be what love is, being sexually abused. When you are that little and sexualized (when a child is imposed on with sexuality) the brain does the best it can to make sense of the situation by associating love with abuse. This becomes "normal" and "common" for all children of any kind of abuse, including emotional and physical abuse, such as beating, etc. When this abuse is mostly what a child knows then it becomes familiarized as "love." This also leads to a kind of trauma bonding where love is fused with pain, and they are seen as one. This causes a person later in life to allow love with abuse and other unhealthy characteristics, thus making the person tolerate too much unhealthiness at their own expense.

I began to feel that I had to monitor the perpetrators' moods and make sure I was not upsetting them, and gauge whether they were in a bad or good mood so that I would know how to proceed to not make it worse. If it was worse for them, it would be worse for me and the other children. I was as good as I could be, and that still did not change their behavior. It might just lessen their angry outbursts.

Trauma bonding is an innate and instinctual bonding that occurs where a victim's only option left is to "bond" with a perpetrator. This is to survive the impact, decrease the suffering, and protect what is left of the core self.

Tragically, for me, as I shared already, it influenced the kind of men I later attracted, which often carried some form of perpetrator characteristics. It took me years to heal the pattering of trauma bonding. These were some of the hardest issues I ever attempted to heal because it was imprinted for so long at a young age. It had become a pattern of my life until I directly addressed it, which took many years. It took years of therapy, perseverance, and patience.

It is up to the frontal brain, our conscious mind, to inform us when a trigger happens and if it is truly dangerous or not. For example, if a bus almost runs you over and your heart rate increases and you shake, this is a normal amygdala response. But if you are trying to decide about taking a supplement and become panicked, this can be an over-reaction of the amygdala triggered into thinking this is a life-or-death situation. To discern this, you can ask:

"Does a part of me feel like this is a life-or-death situation, or more serious than it really is?"

Often when there has been chronic trauma and thus dysregulation, many normal decisions and situations can feel way more serious than they are. It is important for one to then name that this is not so serious, and not life or death. In that way, the amygdala gets informed and can reset to "normal" over time.

Victims live between shifting states of freezing, dissociation, or fight and flight. This terror has become trapped, recycling in the victim's system, and therefore, reinforces the vulnerability of the victim. It locks them into a vicious cycle of entrapment. It can take years for one to interrupt and dismantle the cycle within themselves. And to this day I am still dismantling aspects of the effects of a dysregulated autonomic nervous system.

A dysregulated autonomic nervous system is when the nervous system goes from hyperarousal states to hypoarousal states.

Hyperarousal can look like high pulse rates, manic behavior, moving quickly into overstimulation, insomnia, talking quickly, and shifts to hypoarousal states of freezing, collapsing, fatigue, wanting to sleep, feeling stuck, and inertia.

It can even extend internally, where you feel like your own body may try to kill you through uncontrollable symptoms that are chaotic or even parts of your psyche that you fear may take over and kill you.

The work is cumbersome, deeply layered, and very complex. Most people cannot do it alone, requiring the help of a trained healing professional. Some may suffer from debilitating medical symptomatology as well as panic attacks, phobias, OCD (obsessive-compulsive disorder), multiple personality, schizophrenia, and suicide in some cases.

If you, or anyone you believe is suffering in any one of these states, this is where I offer my connection to you. This is why I am sharing my story with you now. As a community, no one must suffer in silence. We are all connected.

I REALIZED WHAT SERVED ME DURING MY TRAUMA-FILLED YEARS: I UNCONSCIOUSLY DISSOCIATED TO STAY INTACT

When I was repeatedly violated in these acts of ritual sexual abuse in this religious cult, my body container was deeply weakened. Yet, this was paradoxically the strengthening of my energy circuits and abilities which would be used much later as a channel and healer because I had to go up and out of my body and live in the energy realms. I also learned how to access deep trance/altered states for these were so similar to the places that I had to go to survive.

I appeared to move through life like any other person except deeply repetitive, traumatic events were occurring in between with huge memory losses, lapses of time, dissociation, panic attacks, anorexia-bulimia, and suicidal ideation prevailed.

Many other somatic symptoms began to reveal themselves over time in my life. Chronic fatigue and chronic body illnesses, physical and emotional pain, seizures, agoraphobia (fear of leaving home), night terrors, and fear of small spaces and public bathrooms, were just some of the lifelong challenges that began to show up in my life. They were my body telling the story that I had not let out or re-membered yet.

IN MY MOMENTS OF DESPAIR "FIRST LIGHT" APPEARED

I have come to name this kind of grace that occurred for me during these moments of despair as "First Light" – the moments when somehow, somewhere a brush of a hand on my shoulder, a whisper, a breath, a guide, or a crack of light appeared to save me.

Do you know that feeling when you are underwater, and you cannot quite get to the surface fast enough? Those were what my younger years consisted of – lots of deep psychic water, sometimes swimming, navigating, flailing, floating, and not really knowing at times which way was up until First Light appeared.

First Light is like a shimmering crack, a parting in the layers or waves where the light reaches you. Water can be dark, thick, and disorienting. The deeper the water the more likely you may lose your way. Even divers get lost many times underwater, especially when there are caves involved. For me, there were many underwater caves. In this way, the water is like our emotions and unconscious.

Sometimes I would get pulled up and out from that oceanic mess and there would be a reprieve or moment of stillness. What I experienced was profound stillness and gracious light. I would float, hover, and skim above. I could even move freely and effortlessly. While I was dissociated, I was up and out and something much bigger was keeping me alive and intact.

I spent most of the time out of my body and far away somewhere else. You know what it is like when you awaken from a dream, and you can only recall some of it or maybe nothing at first, and sometimes the pieces will often come back in segments and at times it even begins to fade. Well, that is a little of what it is like when you have been dissociated. It feels like you were dreaming and then there is a distant and fuzzy semblance of what occurred, almost like you are viewing and feeling it within a fog and from a distance. There is a feeling of "Did that really happen? Am I making all that up?"

This is exactly what ritual abusers want the victim to experience. They strive in mind controlling to confuse victims and to greatly disorient them so that they no longer know what is real. In this way, naturally a person, especially a child will want to anchor into someone else or believe someone else when in such an extreme state of confusion and disorientation.

These perpetrators attempted to break me, to kill my spirit, and to humiliate and frighten me through heinous acts of violence and sadism. This gives the perpetrators power, control, and release, or the chemical high they are seeking during these violent acts of crime.

The fact that no one around me even noticed this still perplexes me to this day. But when everyone around you is walking around like a war survivor in a thick trauma field, it is to be expected. I guess I covered it up well and everyone around me was also dissociated. I did not dare tell anyone because I thought it was my fault and when I tried, I was shut down by my parents.

The metaphor of the result of the abuse was like being trained to be a CIA agent, covert, numb, disconnected, and tough beyond measure. It is the one, single most thing the ritual abuse had grooved within me: "do not feel, or you will die" … or worse yet, lose yourself by being broken. Through the abuse, my system had been programmed at a young age. I had learned the ability to shut out all feelings and to speak and act dispassionately and flatly in the most intense times. When later in therapy, I would report unspeakable acts of violence that had happened to me to my therapist, I would sound as if I was making a shopping list. The trouble was I had more than one alias within me and in fact, too many to count.

Surviving this and later thriving was truly the beginning of my Shamanic training. This type of abuse was providing me inadvertently with my very training. I learned by leaving my body how to go into deep trance states later in life consciously so that I could channel and receive guidance on behalf of my clients. The power and the wisdom it took to stay alive, sane, and later to thrive were exactly the skills needed to be a shaman. A shaman's job is to transmute heavy energy regularly and sometimes even in the face of near-death experiences. This person is a bridge. I was in deep training for many years through my traumatic life experiences. First light is what kept me alive.

I EXPERIENCED DEEP SUFFERING ONLY TO AWAKEN AND FIND MY PURPOSE IN LIFE

I have a profound, keen interest in what keeps people sane and safe and especially in what returns them to wholeness when they feel they have been splintered (fractured). These very skills and coping mechanisms that save the Self early on when it is not yet fully formed or strong enough to withstand the onslaught of conditioning are exactly the very thing that needs to be dismantled later in life, when the Self is strong enough.

My core Self had gone so far away into such a deep hiding place that it could not be touched by anything. … including myself. Unbeknownst to me at the time, my core was covered by layers of protection and a profoundly wise system of many parts that kept it untouched and therefore whole. All these other parts of my psyche kept me functioning in the best way they could for my well-being. Even so, it was very chaotic and distressing.

This is called Fragmentation or Fracturing.

Who are we when we do not know who is here? Some call that the shadow, or these hidden exiled parts of ourselves. Either we are operating from a fragment(s) of the psyche or from pure awareness. And most of us regularly shift from one to the other.

As I was growing up it seemed my mind was like a large piece of glass that cracked and over time the stresses separated it out until one day it lost its cohesiveness and there was a feeling of being broken into many lost pieces. It felt like a shattering, as if something so big and overwhelming cracked me and I shattered just like glass, perhaps all at once. Of course, it was my mind or psyche that shattered and became fragmented.

Kintsugi is the Japanese art of putting broken pottery pieces back together with gold — built on the idea that by embracing flaws and imperfections, you can create an even stronger, more beautiful piece of art.

The wholeness and vastness, the spirit, that we are can never be touched, not by anything, no matter how heinous or tumultuous.

I became a weaver. It was like I already knew how to bring the parts back together again. And yet it is some of the hardest work I have ever done and am still doing. It was like weaving a blanket together of many patches, threads, and colors. The parts would rebel, hide, attack, freeze, and freak out all at the same time. All that was needed was to allow each to be in its beauty and fullness regardless of the context.

What was needed was understanding, listening, willingness, compassion, direction and so much patience. The trick was not to become identified with a part, nor deny any of them by pushing them away. That is a fine line. In this way, I could help them see and hear each other and learn to work together.

First, I had to be a good parent to the young, fragmented parts of myself and learn how to work with them and help them from my core adult Self. Believe me, though, I did it all, every extreme, but not on purpose. I became them. I pushed them away. I denied them much of the time. I was simply doing the best I could. The intense emotions and unconscious beliefs were so powerful, along with triggers and conditioning, that they would take me over. It was so overwhelming, just like the original experiences of the trauma that had created these feelings now. I was feeling for the first time what I could not process back then when I was so little and incapable of understanding.

I felt like I was a teacher in the rowdiest, gnarliest classroom full of kids who had been through the worst of circumstances. I had no training for how to run this "crazy classroom." So many times, I wanted to give up because the task at hand felt so completely over whelming. I felt totally incapable. I had to take care of all the different parts in the same space, all at the same time inside of me. To say I would get overwhelmed would be an understatement. I felt crazy at times and feared I would go crazy.

I retraced these past events and feelings for the first time, as these child parts were remembering and coming out of the closet. Some of them had been buried or denied for so long that I had to take care and be extremely delicate in being with them. Some of these parts often felt like a wild animal that had been abused for so long that they feared all humans and were shaking and hiding within.

Many times, I did not feel I was up to the task and instead felt as if I was drowning in a sea of confusion, overwhelm, pain, and severe body sensations. Other times during the reintegration work with these parts when there were opposing parts triggered, I would freeze, feel numb, and immobilized with such heaviness and paralysis that I literally could not speak nor move for many hours. It felt like something heavy was on me and I was underwater disappearing from the world. This would usually occur after having been triggered by someone very intimate in my life who had touched a core memory.

This is called "Freezing" and wild animals do it all the time when being pursued in danger, just like the deer in the headlights. This is a response to overwhelming trauma. To exit the freeze took much patience, time, and work. When the freeze would come on, I would say out loud, "I feel frozen." Then I would call Source and ask for help. I would try to touch my body gently or shake slightly or just breathe and eventually the thawing would happen.

Much of the time the voices would be screaming all at once and were uncontrollable. I had extreme fatigue in the mornings during those times and had been diagnosed with chronic fatigue syndrome and adrenal exhaustion for most of my adult years as a result of having been terrified and under attack for so long. My body felt like a heavy weight that I was dragging around and could barely make it through each day. I awoke with an immobilizing weight on my body, and feeling as if I could not rise.

I experienced intense feelings of separation and isolation as I realized early on that most people had not had this breach of the psyche, and that most were not fragmented as far on the continuum as I was. I would become taken over by my emotions and switch from part to part. That came to me with great shame and aloneness at times and would take many years to resolve.

And yet the response I was having was "normal" for the traumatic events I had experienced. It was surprising to some trained professionals that I did not have more noticeable severe symptoms. I had become very good at hiding, numbing, and avoiding. Many other victims who had incurred similar abuse were in mental institutions. Many would adopt multiple personality disorders, self-mutilate, become addicts, or commit suicide.

I did have impulses to commit suicide many times and to harm myself in a self-mutilating way. I resisted these urges. I came to understand why this was happening. My therapist who is a ritual abuse cult specialist and has been working with me for the last several decades explained it to me. It was truly with her help and the guidance of Source that I came to understand that the urges to self-mutilate and of suicide came from my early experiences of not being able to tolerate that level of pain. That very toxic energy that had been forced into me from abuse was stored in my body and it had turned me against my own body. My system had internalized the abuse, and the only place safe to take out that rage and self-hatred in the past had been on my own body. I could not dare act out on the perpetrators, or my parents, or I would be harmed further or abandoned or neglected by my parents.

I had to learn that this was a version of the perpetrator's energy in my body, and I had to release that energy outward through different mechanisms that were healthy. I used running, exercise, dancing, shaking, writing out the anger in my journal, yelling, and consciously out loud role-playing towards the abusers. All these mechanisms helped me keep from harming myself. And truly, my connection to Source is what ultimately kept me from ending my life and from harming my body in other ways. I would feel the light and the faint wispy presence of it around me and the truth of who I am. I was so dedicated to Source, and I could not betray it. It was like hurting myself would be hurting Source. This is one way I stayed intact and sane during the memory retrieval years. There were some intense times when I did not feel like I could go on any longer and I would say "I'm doing this for others" or I would intend that I was doing it for God. That would keep me going. It did not feel enough to do it for myself. It was way too hard. But the thought of doing it for others carried me on.

BLACKNESS COMFORTED ME

The darkness/nighttime did not scare me even as a child. In fact, I was drawn into it craving its dark veil to fall across the day and to nestle upon my shoulders and caress me into black space. As soon as the sun would rest over those rolling Appalachian Hills something within me would also rest.

I found relief in the night and craved her pitch blackness which would envelop me like a blanket of soft black snow. I felt cradled and held by her dark, quiet grace. I trusted her in her fierce, piercing truth. I knew the night would not lie to me and that what I would get would be clear and straight. She was real.

Anything could happen in the daytime as people put on their masks and fed the illusion with facades acting their part. I never remember being sexually abused in the night. It was always in the day. But in the night no one could hide, the veil dropped down, guards lessened and a deep softening and relaxing began, kind of like sinking into deep dark wet waves.

I LEARNED KEY SKILLS IN HEALING MYSELF AND MY CLIENTS: EMPATHY WITH BOUNDARIES IS A KEY TO UNDERSTANDING

Forgiveness came too quickly for me. Being an empath, I could feel everyone's feelings including their pain, *especially* their pain. I did not want anyone to suffer, maybe because I knew what deep suffering felt like.

To this day I work with the fine line between service and over-responsibility and the discernment to not take on the energies of others. This is such a common theme for many deeply compassionate people, especially those who work in the line of service. This can be, for many, a lifelong issue of understanding and creating boundaries.

Where does one draw the line? You can have empathy without taking on the energies, symptoms, and feelings of someone else. If you have been connected to someone and then walk away with their emotions and symptoms, then you know you have gone too far and need to set boundaries.

I am asked by many people how it is possible to completely love oneself, be sovereign, and be there for others? I have found the truth for me. If I am truly loving myself, then any acts that I choose with another will ultimately serve them as well. This is by resonance of vibration, and everything is vibration. This love will then model to others, self-love, and this love ripples out as emanations. I ask myself before moving with a person, "What do I have to offer, truly to offer?"

DEEP LISTENING IS A GIFT YOU CAN GIVE TO OTHERS

Deep listening is a profound and internal process. This is how it can be missed so easily. It can be subtle.

What does it mean to really listen? Where does deep listening emerge? I discovered it comes from the whole light body, like our second skin. It comes from this outer layer, an antenna and receiver of information. The light body that surrounds us becomes like our ears. You may extend your awareness to the space and cocoon of energy around your physical body and listen from that whole space. This has a way of increasing your sensitivity and perceptive ability. In this way, the energy tendrils in your light body become like nerve endings or receptors and begin to perceive/sense what is occurring on many more subtle levels. It is easy to miss listening if you are locating elsewhere in "what's next," in the future, in the thinking mind, or lost in your emotions.

Deep listening dwells in a quieter place within and around you. A helpful question might be: "What might you be missing in your activity and busyness?" It would be like dropping into a deprivation chamber, and suddenly the noises that distract you are gone. What might be left underneath?

Through all these experiences it was my body, specifically my back, which taught me the art of deep listening. I thought I was listening in all my attempts and sincere care for my back, but really, I was unconsciously trying to control it, heal it, and fix it. Mostly my back just wanted to completely unwind, dismantle itself, and release its burdensome memories. It simply needed compassion and tenderness. It became an amazing experience of deconstruction. I learned to simply let it be at times and that was what my back needed the most. Many things had been imposed on that part of my body already. I realized in some unconscious way I had been subtly reenacting this same pattern of trying to get my back to be a certain way and to feel okay, instead of just letting it be and relaxing and breathing into it.

I had to allow a very nonlinear, chaotic process to happen intimately in my body for the "unwinding" to occur. The searing, relentless nerve pain brought me into the present moment like nothing else I had ever experienced. All I could do was be there, and that was no easy task. It was hard to stay present and, in my body, and not feel the intense pain take over me. There was no escape.

116

It was a solo journey and one that no one could really accompany me on, even as kind and supportive as people were to me. No one could go there with me, for I was on such a deep and private terrain by myself. At times, and as you can imagine, there was loving pressure from those around me to pursue various highly invasive medical routes. It was hard for those around me to witness what I was experiencing and to feel so helpless.

In the deep listening, I was clearly guided in exactly what to do. This is not to say that I did not do, nor take things to help my body to be more comfortable, even within the medical realm. I did and was grateful for the assistance. Looking back, I am glad I stayed true to the knowing within me by not having more invasive techniques done to my back. It is clear to me now, that since my pain was mostly trauma-sourced that those treatments could have made my condition worse.

I began to breathe into the pain and relax, listening to what it remembered and needed, and to actively track it, stalking it, by going into the pain all the way. This was a shamanic technique that I cultivated. I gave myself over to it day in and day out, month after month, year after year. I had to let go of wanting to understand why the pain was taking so long to go away.

This became my groundwork for how to really listen to others. It was a great teaching for me which I use in my healing practice. I continue today to deepen in the art of listening, as I have learned there is no end to this deepening.

WE HEAL OURSELVES AND EACH OTHER THROUGH THE ART OF DEEP CONNECTION

Not only does healing require deep listening but I realized healing happens through connection. All of these amazing healers and friends who showed up were the opposite of how the trauma had occurred, in isolation.

This was the opposite of the trauma I had experienced throughout my life. The nature of trauma is that it occurs in isolation with no connection to receiving help.

It takes connection for people to heal. What was once in isolation then can receive the healing light and support of another. When people are traumatized, they are alone without help and need the experience of another to balance/regulate the limbic system back into a soothing centered presence, thus calming the nervous system.

During the art of deep connection, I would ask myself:

- How can I be of service here?
- What am I being asked to see or realize or shift?
- Is there a way I am asleep unto myself and therefore asleep to what is happening in the world or with my loved ones around me?
- How can I make another's life better?"

If another is suffering, then that is one too many. This must come not from a place of responsibility for others but from a place of genuine compassion and support, and of lifting another up. It can be easy to fall into numbness and isolation, as well as in denial, and to be solo, especially in the West.

If we continually ask ourselves: How can we lift each other up? Then what may seem unbearable becomes bearable with the help and support of someone else.

We are not meant to do it alone.

I could not have stayed alive in this life if it was not for the help of the amazing people who came along to support me. My deepest gratitude to my human guides, mentors, friends, and Source. Because of them and other friends and allies, I am alive today to tell my story. Also, I extend a deep thanks to Kelly Clarkson for the song "Stronger" which

I played every day after writing this story for the reminder of how our challenges empower us.

"ISHQ" is a Sufi word for the light and energetic fabric like the love-glue holding us all together. This is a form of the ultimate connection. It is the light matrix or "ether-net" (not referring to the internet technology). This invisible "web of light" that surrounds us all and lives within us is the smallest of particles unseeable to most human eyes. The Sufis call it "Ishq," that which holds the universe together. This is a vast cosmos full of wisdom and information informing us at our every turn if we listen.

> God is love, lover and beloved."
>
> — ISHQ ALLĀH MA'BŪD ALLĀH

Within this field of connection lies all possible answers. The people I needed to heal came into my life when I needed them most. They were answers to my prayers. My advice to anyone suffering is to ask for support, be patient, and not despair.

There was still much uncharted territory for me to discover on my own. Everyone's experience is different and unique. Tools and techniques are wonderful and helped me along the way and yet, no two people are alike in pathological expression regarding healing. It is important to trust your own way. Trusting yourself and your system will show you The Way.

Deep listening and discernment were two of my greatest allies.

I surrendered to Source when I was at a loss for how to heal and it became a constant practice. There were many times when peace was not available amidst the feelings of chaos and inner distress. I found that if I moved into acceptance, there would be a relief and release of energy and more ease flooded my system. It was during these times that I would ask for support and guidance and receive it.

"This is yours, please take it from me. It is too big, and I cannot carry it any longer. Show me the way and bring Grace."

Always, Grace would come as First Light and a door would open. I would soften, relax, and surrender.

> If we have no peace, it is because we have forgotten that we belong to each other."

— MOTHER TERESA

I LEARNED TO LOVE MYSELF THROUGH ALL OF MY BROKENNESS

If someone asked me one of the most important factors for healing and awakening, I would say Self-Love. Placing this first has continued to become paramount in my life and allows me to be present for others and to truly love them. This means to continually turn love towards the self and to be the giver and receiver simultaneously.

As I would give love to others, I would remind myself to give it within. I was naturally inclined to give love to all others, but the remembrance to turn it within was a retraining process.

I realized later that loving myself had been conditioned out of me, and that I had actually been punished when I turned toward myself as a child. Anytime I focused on myself or listened within, I was punished or abandoned by either the perpetrators or my family, so I learned very quickly to vacate myself and focus entirely on caring for others because it would keep me safer. My parents certainly had no ability to nourish me or comfort me, so I did not get the appropriate modeling from them as well of how to do that for myself.

In my years as a healer, I have met many others who were burdened with this similar experience.

Naming how hard and messy the process was became a very helpful and necessary tool, which gave me permission to relax and allow it all to unfold. Welcoming it all became the path of least resistance and only then would ease and comfort become available to me.

I BEGAN TO REASSOCIATE AND TRUST MYSELF AND OTHERS

When there is overwhelming trauma, the shattering, you see, is essential. It is the way the core self becomes protected and stays intact. The core self goes into hiding and is covered by the fragmented parts. The core self remains buried until there is enough resourcing, stability, and grounding within the person for them to reassociate (come back together again).

These disparate parts of diverse ages organize most effectively to keep the person functioning and thus protected as well as possible. The internal parts are like lost children who are too young for such responsibilities (making decisions in life, etc.). They often had insufficient healthy, appropriate role models, so they made it up as best they could to help the person survive.

The parts do this as long as they must until the strength and ability emerge from the core for them to heal. There must be a readiness and capacity within the person to be able to acknowledge and feel certain levels of intense memory and emotions from the traumas that created the parts in the first place.

Most of the time this initial work of reassociation cannot be done alone but requires the assistance of a trained professional. This is because most traumas happen when one is alone and isolated during these experiences. Often the overwhelm of the events is too much for a traumatized person to re-pattern alone and requires the help of another. This, being assisted by another and being limbically regulated by them, and thus not feeling alone, can help heal much of the trauma. When a limbically regulated or calm, centered person with a balanced nervous system sits with a traumatized person the victim can learn to regulate through a beautiful syncing process that happens over time.

Often one of the challenges that arises is that these parts are so accustomed to being alone that they do not know how to trust, much less receive another's help. And this trust can take some time to reestablish. This also depends upon spiritual timing with sufficient external and internal support for the reintegration process to begin. Depending on the extent, depth, age, and length of the childhood trauma this could take years.

The truth is that all people have "parts" to some greater or lesser extent. The human experience of initial separation and living in duality itself is traumatizing and most people have some fragmented and compartmentalized parts to some level.

Most people without heavy childhood trauma have the core self more accessible. The gaps between their parts are less, and the autonomy of each part is not as distinctly developed. This makes the separateness less defined and less influential in the person's whole system. For people with fragmentation, the gap and separation are huge, and it is like trying to cross the sea without a bridge.

These parts can take over for long periods and run the show without the person realizing what is occurring. I call this getting "hijacked" or being taken over and it leads to another form of a trance state.

Once enough internal muscle is built within the core self, a stepping back process can be used, a kind of detachment, (by locating one's awareness in the background) and from this place witnessing the foreground of emotions. I call this state, "witnessing awareness." It can be helpful to ask a question like:

"Who is having these feelings?"

"How old is the one who is having these feelings?"

Then attempt to access that part of yourself who has those feelings.

The choice can be, "Do I wish to live in the vastness of myself or the smallness"? You can consciously choose to shift into greater awareness or be pulled into a small, fragmented part. And the truth is that sometimes at first, we cannot control it. When we identify with a young part of ourselves, that is where the suffering can be. There is no judgment in either, as we switch between these places all the time. It is a natural process.

THE IMPORTANCE OF UNDERSTANDING WHAT TRANCES ARE AND HOW THEY IMPACT US

Trances have a way of making one feel very focused within a narrow bandwidth where anything in the general overview or periphery becomes unnoticeable temporarily. These types of trances happen when we are identified with the egoic parts of ourselves. It can take some time to rebuild the muscle of the core self. It is like going to the gym and working out a muscle that has not been used for some time. It may even be that one was punished by others for being true to themselves in their core and so coming back into it again may bring up feelings of fear or shame or wrongness or simply unfamiliarity and awkwardness.

One of the tricky aspects is to be able to locate in awareness and witness these places without abandoning them because they need compassion and presence. Often, they have been alone and separated for so long. **I have not found meditation to be enough to integrate them at times.** The active force of loving and "being with" them is needed. It is not our role to leave them, nor judge them, but to simply be present with them and to turn love within towards the self.

SELF-SOOTHING IS A TECHNIQUE I HAVE FOUND ESSENTIAL DURING MY HEALING JOURNEY

There is a way of not leaving, nor indulging and merging with the small self. It is a fine line. I will often place my hands on my body and gently rub my hands across my skin in a soothing manner. I call this self-soothing, and I will offer the younger parts of myself very nourishing and comforting words. This also creates the lovely biochemical of oxytocin, which makes us feel happy and peaceful.

In those moments I would simply be with the overwhelming emotion and try not to do anything, but simply hold this part of myself and rock it like a child. Sometimes this uncomfortable feeling can last a while. My only job when this would occur in my healing was to bear the pain, stay with it, and know it would pass. Often, I would say simple phrases to myself like "You're OK. I know it doesn't feel like it but you're really OK." "This is going to pass." Sometimes these gentle reminders like a parent would say to their child were exactly what was needed and missing. I always called in Source for help, and it never failed me. Bearing my pain with presence and love was enough. Sometimes it is all you can do. Be patient. Soon, it will transform. The Light of your consciousness will transform it.

In those moments of intensity, it can seem like forever, even though it is only hours or days or weeks. That is often how intense trauma feels in the moment when it is occurring, like it's never going to end. So, when you are healing it and touching that old trauma, it may feel that way too. But it will end. Remember that it is okay to float. Sometimes you just float. This does not mean that it will not change. When you suffer from childhood sexual trauma or any kind of chronic trauma, the level of fragmentation, that deafening noise within can be overwhelming. The draw can feel like a strong ocean undertow pulling you into a drowning feeling deep and under, again and again. Just like in the ocean in an undertow, sometimes the best way through is to float and stop fighting the current until another stream arises of pure flow. You may find yourself cast off from shore, and out to sea, before catching the current that will bring you back. The vast ocean will never desert its waves. She will always bring you home.

THE GIFT OF THE BODY~A SOMATIC TECHNIQUE FOR COMING HOME

So much had been done to my body that for a long time, I wasn't very good at even feeling it, much less being present in it. I had shut that mechanism off so that I could cope. But ironically, it's exactly what I needed in order to ground and feel calm. I needed to come home. I had to do deep retraining to be able to feel sensations and different parts of my body. Eventually, this became a refuge where I could simply focus on a part of my body and the sensations I felt, and I could allow my consciousness to dwell there. This had a great calming effect, and I would use it whenever my mind got too busy or scared or when I felt out of control or disconnected. I would pick a part of my body, drop in, and feel the sensations, especially in my lower body since I had been up and out so much. I would ground and connect my feet and my seat to the Earth and really feel my connection below my body to gravity holding me. And I would say "I'm being held by something so much bigger than me. This earth nourishes and feeds me and is so vast and even holds me in place with gravity." I would allow the mothering of the earth to rise around me, and really feel her support.

This beautiful exercise came to me during that time. If you wish, close your eyes, take a couple of deep breaths, and allow your mind simply to drop down and rest in your heart. Breathe in and out slowly feeling the rise and fall of your rib cage and diaphragm. If your mind becomes busy, you can simply witness the train moving by without jumping on. Then come back to your heart, resting in your heart. After a couple of minutes of resting here, move your attention and focus on your deep belly and simply feel sensations in your body, noticing where they are. Simply breathe into that area and allow it to relax even more deeply. If you feel any pain or resistance, welcome it, move towards it, and allow it to be just as it is. You may wish to breathe a little more deeply into this area and allow light to come in on the inhale funneling it into this part of your body. On your exhale you may wish to release any pain, distress, or heaviness. Rest here as long as you wish, allowing deep, calm, and relaxation. Then gently rubbing your hands over your legs and over your arms in a soothing manner, you can say "I am here, I am here."

I WAS PROTECTED, DEFENDED, AND REDIRECTED

I was always enamored with folklore, nature, and the outdoors. I knew a Phoenix rises from the ashes. But I often wondered who would lift me if I did not have the strength to rise. At times, I felt like there were invisible hands all around me cradling me and lifting me. I was protected.

Many times, it was not up to me. I had given up. At times I felt this vast force of love. It was not the crazy, romantic kind but the all-pervading kind like you would perceive between a good parent and a child.

During my reassociation time, I had a magical event occur. My whole life I had felt like my birth name. "Lara" was not quite my name. One rainy day, I sat down on my meditation cushion, closed my eyes, and entered the deep silence, as I always did. I asked Source, please reveal to me my true name.

I sat in silence for a while, resting, and relaxing, having learned to not reach for an answer, or expect anything to happen in my own human timing. To my surprise, not long into the meditation, I heard a voice whisper to me "Isa."

The voice continued whispering this name, which I had never heard before. I was in deep gratitude for the guidance coming through, but I knew I would not change my name so quickly without more reassurance. Even as I learned to accept my role as a shaman, which was not quick, and quite skeptical, I always sat with the information I received. I let it simmer and sit with me.

The next day I sat again on the deep purple cushion on which I had sat for so many years and asked. I heard "Isa" again. I repeated this for several days and got the same response. Somehow this relieved me. It was a big decision to change my name. It was part of my identity and held transformative significance. I knew I could trust the name that was being given to me.

Sometime later when I traveled to Maui, I met with a spiritual friend and scholar. When I shared my new name with him, his eyes lit up and he said, "Do you know what Isa means? I said, "No, I had never really thought about it before." I just knew it was given to me from Source and I validated it many times. He proceeded to tell me that it was the mother text of the Upanishads, holy Vedic Scripture. I became very curious. This time I did my research. I was astonished at what I found:

Isa Upanishad

OM

Purnamadah Purnamidam

Purnat Purnamudachyate

Purnasya Purnamadaya

Purnameva Vashishyate

OM

The translation is:

"That is the whole.

This is the whole.

From wholeness, emerges wholeness.

wholeness coming from wholeness.

Wholeness still remains."

This had been my entire life: what I had been working towards reclaiming my wholeness, and feeling whole again from all the fracturing, like shattered glass that had lived within my psyche for so long. Source had given me a name that carried the medicine of exactly what I needed to bring the healing. This had been my life's work to learn how to reweave the coherency of my psyche back together into full integration and to share this gift with others for their healing. I felt this mantra was carrying me, and I felt deeply and humbly grateful to the divine Source for always guiding me and caring for me just like I know it does for you.

TODAY, I AM ABLE TO SERVE OTHERS AS A SHAMAN AND HEALER WITH PASSION AND A DEEP PURPOSE TO HELP OTHERS LIVE THEIR DESTINY

In healing myself, I learned many practices, a few of which I have already shared with you. There are several more here I believe will help you embark on any journey you wish to take, especially in finding your purpose in life. We know when we seek our purpose, we may feel lost, and often lonely, wondering what life has in store for us. My aim here is to show you that you do have a purpose here and to help you see the blessings.

HOW TO GET IN TOUCH WITH YOUR EMOTIONS, NAME THEM, AND BE IN THE MOMENT

It seems like such a simple thing to know how to feel your emotions, but the truth in our modern culture is that many people have been conditioned to push those down. Others were never allowed to feel emotions as children and perhaps were even judged, punished, or abandoned for showing their feelings or trained later in life to turn it off, valuing getting things done more than being and feeling.

In some ways "doing" has become a mass trance and feelings get in the way. But the right action comes out of a deeper place, of tuning in or sensing within. There is no time to feel if you are compulsively busy, in survival, and constantly living for the future. As one learns to pause and listen within, stirring from a deeper place arises. Being present in the now can happen. This allows a shift into the re-balance of the masculine and feminine.

Here is an invitation to suspend your mind, by asking it to step back or quiet down for just a moment while you try something new. You can clear the slate of your mind as if you are erasing a chalkboard. Imagine you might not know how to feel your emotions. Then sense a bit deeper within and in the spirit of fun and lightness see what happens if you approach this as you might have never done it before.

AN EXERCISE IN ALLOWING YOUR FEELINGS TO RISE UP AND NAME THEM

Locate yourself in a quiet, undisturbed place where you feel safe. Closing your eyes, simply experience your body being met by the surfaces around you and feel the sensations of your body. Take some deep breaths. Inhale at the same rhythm or count to your exhale. Deeply relax into your body even more. Allow tension to be released. Now if there is any focus in your head move this into your heart. Let the mind go. Do not follow it. Let your mind rest in your heart. If thoughts come through, let them go and breathe back into the heart. As you soften even more, allow your energy to expand and be curious about how you feel emotionally. You may notice "flavors of emotion," whether subtle or strong.

Emotional numbness may be mistaken for peace. This can be very tricky to discern. Simply notice the qualities present, such as joy, fear, sadness, irritation, anger, discouragement, or any gradations in between. The feelings may be strong or very subtle and sometimes unknown for some time.

Be patient. Practice and give it some time. By giving it practice, the space is enough to bring awareness and relaxation for the unknown to arise. Automatic conditioning may arise bringing the illusion of "I feel fine" or" everything is okay". And of course, you may feel that too.

Here are some helpful ways to tell the difference between emotion and disconnection:

Numbness is a disconnect and requires repression, tension, and contraction. Simply said, it requires energy.

Peace is all-inclusive of everything. It is patient, expansive, spacious, relaxing, and does not require energy.

ONCE YOU CAN FEEL EMOTION YOU CAN PRACTICE THE ART OF EMPATHY: EMPATHY IS THE KEY TO CONNECTEDNESS

Researchers have studied empathy for years. At first, they thought it was something people were simply born with, either you had it, or you didn't. Now, we know that is not true. You can learn how to become more empathic.

We are a social species and depend on each other for love, nurturing, support, and comfort. As I mentioned at the beginning of my book, a newborn's entry into this world begins a pattern of significant development – on every level - and is critical to their upbringing.

Empathy enables us to share experiences and desires and serves as an emotional bridge. In a nutshell, it is like asking: Can you feel me? Or for starters can you feel yourself? This is what many people are in need of without even realizing it. I call this the "art of empathy." Can you really know what someone else is going through? How can you get as close to what they are experiencing as possible without taking it on, so that you can be truly with them?

As an empath one is aware of what someone is feeling whether "the other" has shared it with you verbally or not. It is like an extra sense. It's a little hard to put into words. I have always had it for as long as I can remember and used to think when I was younger that all humans had it too, but I quickly realized that everyone did not. I discovered that some people had not yet cultivated their empathy or simply did not know what it was. Just hearing, seeing another, or being near someone I could feel what was happening inside of them and it was even amplified if I were to touch the person. I would become acutely aware of what was occurring in their body, emotions, and mind in some general way.

Human beings are unique in their soul, personality, gifts, challenges, karma, and destiny. We cannot really know what a person has been through or how they have been influenced. Therefore, it is important to be humble and listen deeply to one another, with kindness.

When I am with my clients and engaging in the art of empathy, I might ask myself:

- What have you come here to do?
- What are your lessons?
- What must you fulfill?
- What are your gifts?

Usually, one will feel their mission as an urging or a soul pressure in the energy field, something wanting to burst through the layers and be anchored within and embodied. It can also be felt as an urge in the physical body. Source seeks expression in many ways through all of us. It is how consciousness experiences itself in form. Many creations are seeking birth on earth and have chosen a particular soul for the fulfillment of these unique creative expressions.

Even if you are not an empath, you can truly listen to another and imagine what the person is experiencing. It is important to put yourself in another person's shoes, pause, and give someone the benefit of the doubt that they might be having a hard time or struggling through something, even if they are acting out.

If you truly know how another feels, then it is easier to have compassion and not make them an enemy.

AN EXERCISE IN PRACTICING EMPATHY TO INCREASE CONNECTEDNESS

A great exercise is to close your eyes and imagine something that another is feeling, something charged or intense, and what that might be like given their history and life circumstances. Now imagine this happening to you but with their background, circumstances, and their wiring. You may or may not fully be able to feel it. But the very act of empathy births a world with more kindness and peace.

Of course, we are all wired differently and have different experiences, and karma that shape us i.e. unique family lineages, destinies, etc. Yet there is still some similarity in sharing, even if you cannot understand how or why someone is feeling one way or another. This can be a good practice to learn from them and to open and honor their experiences. We can learn so much from each other if we are curious and stay open.

To feel another, honor them, and have compassion is an act of creating peace.

In an empath's journey, it is possible to polish your skills by not taking on other's energies, nor taking on the suffering of the world. You can feel others and know the difference between yourself and others. There are many powerful energy medicine and shamanic techniques to assist this.

IN PRACTICING EMPATHY, YOU WILL NEED TO SET BOUNDARIES

In a spiritual sense, we are all one and there is no separation. And yet in these earthly psychological and energetic realms, it is important to know where one begins and another ends, at least as a stepping stone to be able to embody oneself safely and harmoniously. This is what is known as boundaries. If the strength of your energy field and expansion is big enough, then all other frequencies may dissolve in this contact and no sticking will occur.

As an empath, it is unusual to not know what someone is feeling. My empathic channel was so strong I had to work on toning it down to stay in balance and function in a sovereign way. Then I could maintain my own energy field without taking on responsibility for others and transmuting their pain through my body. I would walk down the street, pass someone who was in enormous pain, and then feel a deep visceral pain in my stomach which would almost knock me down. The emotional pain would be so overwhelming that sometimes I would weep and try to figure out how to help the person. This is a lovely gesture but one cannot go all around all day living from this place. This creates depletion and imbalance.

This took me many years of consistent training to release the habit of taking on other energies. When I was violated repetitively in the past, my energetic and physical boundaries were constantly knocked down, so I became conditioned to drop my energy boundaries. I became so porous and psychically open that I took on everything around me and was like a psychic vacuum cleaner. I became sick from doing it. By the time I met Leta Rose, I was very toxic from taking on other energy. Our early work together was emptying me out from all this collective heavy debris and bringing my energy back to me.

PRACTICING THE ART OF EMPATHY CAN CHANGE THE WORLD

Perhaps If we all practice the art of empathy, violence might lessen. Can you imagine this being taught in our schools, The Art of Empathy, and how things would change?

When one tries on what another one is feeling, as if it is their own, it creates a deep connection of compassion and bridges separation. It also makes it very difficult to see the other as separate or different. It is then hard to see that person as an enemy. You may realize that God is being reflected to you in everyone and everything as yourself. This would result in "Why would you ever harm another on purpose if they are you?"

YOU CAN RAISE YOUR VIBRATION AND BECOME A POSITIVE ENERGY INFLUENCE

Everything is frequency and vibration.

All things transmit frequencies, consciously or unconsciously. It is important to know what will lift up your vibration and what will lower your vibration. In more basic terms, it will help you to understand what makes you feel better and what makes you feel worse. To clarify a bit further I am not talking about feeling better in a simply emotional or physical way but truly as a state of being, more whole and integrated and in the right relationship with oneself and everything else. It is not about a quick fix.

In general, on the planet, we are moving into more and more lightness and away from heaviness or density. Our bodies are changing in cellular structure from carbon base to crystalline structure. This does not happen overnight. In this shift, we are releasing patterns of density and toxicity.

Bodies that go through trauma are vulnerable to becoming receptacles for heaviness, both energetically and physically because that is the frequency of the density of trauma and until healed it magnetizes more. Trauma is heavier than normal energy. Trauma crowds the space within the energy field and the physical body until it is released. It also provides plenty of triggers that can range from visual, auditory, olfactory, touch, kinesthetic, and so on, that can be activated at any moment depending on the circumstances. This is why it makes it more difficult for people who have had heavy trauma to move through the world. There are many opportunities for these triggers to become activated. To lessen the suffering it is imperative that these memories and emotions be worked with so that they can be felt, transmuted, and released so that the person can have more freedom and ease moving through life.

If you want to be all that you can be, then you can steer clear of those things that lower your vibration and choose the ones that raise your vibration. Another way to approach this is to discern what dissipates or wastes your chi (energy) which would be felt as a type of drain and what helps you gather and acquire more energy, thus feeling nourished and supported.

FORGIVENESS: FORGIVE YOURSELF FIRST AND TAKE YOUR TIME

Ultimate forgiveness is one of the most important and freeing acts that we may ever do. It is very important not to rush this action.

Forgiveness is not believing that anything that was done to you is okay. It is simply the act of freeing yourself from bondage and entanglement with another soul. When you stay in a state of blame and feel angry you are energetically bound to another or the situation and therefore a prisoner. When you release yourself from this bondage you are empowered. Trust that you will forgive when you are ready. You are essentially freeing yourself from the pain and heavy feelings.

Sometimes you may love someone, and they may just not be healthy enough to have a relationship with or connection at all. It does not mean that you allow them in your space or even necessarily speak to them again. You will be guided and can trust yourself as to what your appropriate relations are to be with someone. In the end, it simply means that you have freed yourself from the entanglement of blame, which ultimately drains your energy.

First, the feelings need to be felt completely on all levels for as long as it takes. I cannot reiterate enough that it may take a very long time to appropriately come into forgiveness. In no way should you push yourself thinking that you should be forgiving when you are not naturally feeling forgiveness. Take all the time you need to go through the normal feelings of blame and rage and upset. It takes psychological integration time and a higher understanding to forgive. Before you can embrace forgiveness, it is helpful to express the feelings living in the body, so they do not get repressed and stored in the tissues.

AN EXERCISE IN PRACTICING FORGIVENESS

Here is a helpful exercise to practice forgiveness.

Start with forgiving yourself. Notice if there is any way you have blamed yourself. Next, allow everything to move through you that you need to feel, say, write, and express. Only then can you tune in and discern if you are still holding on to blame or if you need more time to process the anger and upset. This process in some instances could take months or years.

These questions may help free you:

- What was my soul meant to learn from the situation?
- Is this feeling of blame depleting my energy?
- Is there more I need to feel and express in order to be free?
- How can I retrieve my power here?

ON DISCOVERING YOUR PURPOSE IN LIFE

I hear the question regularly "What is my purpose? I see so many people suffering, and not feeling that they have a sense of purpose or knowing what that is. People endlessly search for how to find their purpose and wind up in jobs or careers they may take just to make ends meet. But nothing moves their soul.

As a Healer I work with many things that I am called by Source to move, bring forth, or bridge. I also function as a medium for any soul's suffering. You could say I have a contract to be in service to these souls. I must speak for those who have no voice or who no one knows may even exist. The trick of course is not to take on such energies or realities but instead to offer energy, support, and light to their cause. We all have a role and serve life in some way.

When I am called by Source to serve in this way, I ask these questions:

- What does life want from me?
- How can I serve life?
- What can I offer life?
- What am I here to learn?
- What is my gift?

The question for a life of fulfillment may not be so much what one can get from life, but what one can offer life. If you get quiet enough and drop below the busyness of the mind it is easier to hear this call. This is what I call, finding your purpose.

There can be much interference to heeding your call. If you sit in the center long enough to let the dust settle from the busy internal chatter of your mind and let the voices in your head take a back seat, then answers and peace can arise. You may receive *inner* direction which arises beyond thinking and having to figure it out by yourself. This arising wisdom shows you the way. It often feels like a nudge, a curiosity, or a pull in a certain direction. At times it is as if you just know to get up and go call that person or do that particular action.

As part of my mediumship, when I am deep in my work trance space tuning in for a client, I often feel/hear the lost suffering soul's voices shuffling in the space around, hovering like ghosts looking for some-thing. I offer kindness and light. I realize the inseparable thread of connection between us, and I acknowledge myself and the One within them. I hold them as I hold myself.

What more can one do beyond shining light where there is darkness within and without? It is not about the outcome, but rather about the quality, the presence, and that moment. Everything is a complete universe within itself, each moment an eternity of now. Presence speaks, and our job is to listen.

I never know if I will be here past the moment because death still lives on my left shoulder, and I feel I need to stay as awake as possible.

I often ask myself two key questions:

Am I awake?

Am I here? I mean here, fully?

Everything is a letting go, birth and death, and everything in between. Every moment comes and goes with diverse states, people, places, and things.

Remember, wherever your attention is going most of the time, is what you are serving, whether consciously or not.

This land of flux and flow is where universes are made within black stars of tiny matter, waiting to explode with their fiery passion for the creation of life. We are being asked to dance. We are all doing it uniquely within this mass of the matrix of life. Do not think you are not needed nor important - ever.

You make up a cell of the whole organism dancing as one, and all cells are needed and unique. Without you, it is harder for someone else to do their job. There is a missing connector and a gap.

Do not hide if your inner voice says, "I cannot do it as another does." Show the world how you dance and teach us a thing or two. Because what you know is not like anyone else among us. Give us a chance to see you and learn from you. Share it, live it, and celebrate what you are – we will show up to support you.

WHATEVER YOU DO CHOOSE TO DO IT AS A MASTER WITH IMPECCABILITY

The clients I have witnessed with the most suffering are often the ones who had to fragment the most to survive. Because of their circumstances, their psyche had to split, and the core had to leave their body in order to protect itself. And so often, they are left with chronic, unexplainable mind and body symptoms, which appear as undiagnosable illnesses. This and many other challenges in life can be the fuel for mastery.

The work of a master is not so much to be happy with an easy, perfect life, but to make peace, come into deep acceptance, and turn into gold what you are presented, no matter how difficult or complex. It is easy to be happy with a relatively, pleasant existence, but the real work is to make peace with the most difficult things in life, to turn them into gifts, and to find joy in this messy process called life. You can polish that gem and offer your tremendous gift to the world through love.

Another aspect of mastery is the commitment to do only what is one's truth, regardless of any outside influences, beliefs within, fear of ridicule and to even risk the loss of love and approval, for belonging is such a deep human need. This means risking pressure from peers, family, society, and even the critic within who has developed inner strategies to keep one "safe". This means at times feeling uncomfortable and out on a limb and risking personal comfort for the truth.

> I tore myself away from the safe comfort of certainty, because of my love for truth, and truth rewarded me."

> — SIMONE BEAUVOIR

MY SOUL KNEW WHAT I DID NOT KNOW, AND I AM BLESSED WITH MY NEW LIFE

For the past 32 years, I have dedicated my life to healing, to helping all things to come back into wholeness again, and to alleviating any suffering. I am still learning more about this every single day. A couple of decades ago, I knew that I made it through the crux of this when new memories would still arise occasionally, but they would not "take me out." I also knew I had made it when strong emotions would flood my body but somehow, I would not lose my sense of adult core

139

self and maintained the ability to move from that deep center of knowing.

The healing journey for me over the last several years has been a continuum of gaining strength, awareness, and the ability to maintain equilibrium. There have been stages where I am flooded again with some old issue or memory that needs to be healed on a deeper level but what remains is a deeper level of strength and awareness and a container with which I am able to meet it. For me now, this ends up looking more like a passing moment instead of a hurricane. Healing still happens and I do not think it will ever stop because we are infinite spirit beings visiting these bodies on the Earth for a temporary time. I have come to believe through my experiences that we are here to learn lessons and evolve. What I am clear about is that what kept me going in the past was my love for Source and my commitment to become all that I am capable of so that I can serve and help other people.

I do know that life will keep delivering whatever is needed for us as souls to experience. I also know we have an opportunity here to awaken to the best version of ourselves as infinite beings, that we have incredible capability and that truly, anything is surmountable. When you remember that, you can draw on the strength that is bigger than yourself and allow the universe to carry you. You never have to do it alone. You can speak to the universe even through the word of prayer, and I do not mean that in a religious sense. You can just talk to the universe. This is an incredible tool to place your intention into the vast space of the universe and say what you wish for and allow it to come to you. This openness and receptivity will draw unto you whatever medicine is necessary for your soul. There is an incredible Great Mystery that is carrying you and listening and here in benevolence to support you.

I HAVE BEEN A PRACTICING SHAMAN, MEDIUM, AND CHANNEL FOR OVER THIRTY-TWO YEARS

Also, during these 32 years, I have been working in my shamanic private practice as a medium, channel, energy medicine healer, and body-centered counselor. My work is to be a bridge for people between the spirit realm and this realm - to be an intermediary between the two worlds. This is so that people can have an experience of the unseen realms, the guidance available here, the power, and the tools available to support them.

There is vast information and wisdom that comes from within each of our beings and you can learn how to listen to and access it. It has been my life's work and still now it is my passion. I teach other people how to access their intuition, knowing, their own inherent language of light and shamanic skills, energy medicine, and channeling ability. This is not some kind of *New Age woo-woo* application but very grounded spiritual techniques in which everyone is inherently capable. People channel all the time without even knowing it.

I am excited to help others to remember these inherent healing skills. Everyone has these abilities living inside of them. It is not something magical or phenomenal. Sometimes these tools just need to be awakened and remembered. I want to empower others with the ability to heal themselves and to help each other.

I see private clients remotely and in person. I also do group transmissions for people where I channel different frequencies of healing energies which I call Prayer Field Healing groups. I teach energy medicine to individuals and groups. I help people remember the chakra and vast energy system and the language of light of where we are all from before we incarnate in a body as pure energy and consciousness. I teach ancient shamanic practices to help people remember how to elicit the power of the natural world and unseen realms. This includes how to see and experience your own light body, to maintain and cleanse the light body, gather, and retain energy, and how to notice how you lose energy.

Mostly, I love assisting others in becoming more aware of and orienting as spirit in a body, remembering their true inherent nature and how to recover your energy from "the world." This includes helping others to bring back parts of themselves that have gone into hiding or exile. I am dedicated to assisting in "remembering," how to re-assemble and bring back together disconnected incoherent parts of self. I also help people shift their attention to the inner space within so they can attend and see what is here and have more peace. This gives you the ability to fulfill your dreams and destiny.

As a seer, I look to see what is in someone's Lightbody and being and what you are carrying. Then I simply move energy to help a person access more balance and well-being. Mostly I sit with others in compassion, listening, presence and allow what really wants to come forth to be seen, felt, and heard, and cared for with great nourishment. Sometimes all you need is a grounded loving presence, sincerely for Grace to come.

> I wish I could show you when you are lonely or in darkness, the astonishing light of your own being."
>
> — HAFIZ

SOURCE GUIDED ME TO GO PUBLIC WITH MY MESSAGE AND CREATE MY MINISTRY ORGANIZATION

In the last several years, I was guided by Source to go public for the first time. I had always done my private practice by word-of-mouth. I was grateful to be able to have such a beautiful, full practice of lovely clients and somewhat stay invisible, and certainly not in the public eye. I was often referred to in my small town as the hermit healer on the hill. I relished this time because it kept my life simple, but as Source would have it, some years ago, I was guided to create a website for the first time and to go public with my work. I am now sharing my story with the world in hopes it might help others.

To fulfill this very endeavor I created Eternal Grace Ministry, my spiritual organization and ministry which is dedicated to bringing healing to the world and helping people wake up to their true nature and re-member themselves back together again. It is our intent to assist in the evolution of human consciousness by helping people uncover and release any limitations, beliefs, memories, or stored traumas from the body, mind, and spirit. We commit to this service through humility, devotion, and honor of each person's inherent worth, equality, and sovereignty. We honor each person as a divine ray of light of consciousness.

Eternal Grace Ministry wishes for anyone in need of healing, or who is suffering in any way to be able to receive healing work. My ministry receives tax-deductible donations which go towards the scholarship fund for those in need to receive different kinds of healing work. Our dedication is also to educate people about the nature of different kinds of abuse with the intention that this will help all abusive behavior cease. The goal is for more people to become aware of the signs and symptoms of abuse, which will, in turn, hopefully help iden-tify victims and help them recover more quickly. The true desire is, of course, to prevent these abusive acts from occurring.

YOU ARE LIGHT EMANATING

When the light gets in, it will move you, and you will know it. A freedom arises. It is as if a tight shoe is taken off and space and new possibilities open. When free of restrictions, adhering to ideas and social norms, freedom ensues.

Faith is not settling for less. Faith is knowing there are infinite possibilities, especially if you cannot see them in the moment. Faith is knowing the best will come to you even if it doesn't seem that way.

Where there is faith, there is a crack for the light to shine. It is knowing everything is just as it is meant to be and **all will be okay**. It becomes apparent that events are just events, and all is ultimately well. It is trusting in the Divine perfection in every moment and allowing the next moment to unfold without knowing the outcome. It makes room for the Divine. This is how the light gets in.

Understandings, creative solutions, or simply pure acceptance may arise from this place. Deep wisdom is a result when the light gets in. When the light gets in you can feel, breathe, and energy can move. When the light gets in you may realize you are more than what you thought you were. I have come to learn over the past three decades:

Who you are is unique and no one else has those qualities or gifts you are here specifically to bring.

If you could see who you really are... **YOU** in your expansive light body, you would be astonished. You are astonishing! The pure potency of your own soul is beyond anything you can imagine. The pure power of your own being is extraordinary.

You have legions of Angels around you guiding your every step along the way.

First Light is awaiting you.

RESOURCES FOR FURTHER ILLUMINATION ON THESE TOPICS

Malidoma Some'

Bessel van der Kolk~ Book: **The Body Keeps the Score: Brain, Mind, and Body in the Healing of Trauma**

Pete Walker, MA~ Book: **"Complex PTSD: From Surviving to Thriving"**

Dan Siegel ~**Book: The Developing Mind: How Relationships and the Brain Interact to Shape Who We Are**

Peter A. Levine and Anne Frederick ~ **Waking the Tiger: Healing Trauma**

Lenore Terr ~ Too Scared to Cry and Unchained Memories

ACKNOWLEDGEMNTS

Through experience, I realize that it is by the grace and help of others that so many aspirations, hopes and dreams get fulfilled. I have many amazing souls to thank regarding this endeavor.

Paul David Renker ~ My dear beloved partner, thank you for the countless hours of positive encouragement, patience, holding, and your enduring committed love.

Lori Lorenz, MA~ My mentor, colleague, and friend, thank you for relaying the truth and understanding of the unfathomable, for the flourishing of my soul, and for your steadfast wisdom and support all these years. You are invaluable.

Alexandra McDermott~ my editor and through this process, my new dear friend, whose relentless positivity, lifting me up, and astounding wisdom and organizational skills were my bridge through the word to this world. Thank you for teaching me how to speak to the world.

Ixchel Tucker~my webmaster, assistant, and friend who handled everything else in between to keep it all running.

You the Reader~ Thank you for who you are and your unique path in life. Without your receiving of this story, there would be no reason for it to be.

Without each of you and your amazing soul gifts, patience, and constant support this book would not have come to be. Thank you all immensely for the encouragement, reminders, and relentless positivity that this story could be put into words.

Thank you to all forces and beings seen and unseen and to the Holy One.

ABOUT THE AUTHOR

Isa Lara Marié is the founder and ordained minister of Eternal Grace Ministry, dedicated to the healing and awakening of all. She has served as a channel and healer in service to All That Is for over 32 years. Isa offers energy medicine/shamanic work, channeling, mediumship, and body-centered counseling. Her training includes 27 years of studying with a mystic and shaman as well as Hakomi certification from founder Ron Kurtz, and many other body-centered healing modalities. Her work is a blend of the Toltec shamanic lineage, along with angelic/galactic guidance. Isa offers in-person, as well as remote healing sessions and teaches energy medicine/shamanic trainings and prayer field healing groups.

Website: IsaLaraMarie.com

www.ingramcontent.com/pod-product-compliance
Lightning Source LLC
LaVergne TN
LVHW051126080426
835510LV00018B/2261